Daily Telegraph

GUIDE TO INCOME TAX

Completely updated edition

prepared by

David B. Genders, F.C.A.

A partner in Sayers Butterworth, Chartered Accountants

COLLINS

LONDON AND GLASGOW

William Collins Sons & Co. Ltd.
London & Glasgow

First published 1974
Completely revised and reset edition 1977
Completely revised and reset edition 1978
Fully updated edition 1979
Completely revised and reset 1980
Fully updated edition 1981
Fully updated edition 1982
Fully updated edition 1983
Completely revised and reset 1984
Fully updated edition 1985

ISBN 0 00 434138 4
Printed in Great Britain

ACKNOWLEDGEMENT
The Inland Revenue forms reproduced in this book are Crown copyright and are reproduced with the permission of the Controller of Her Majesty's Stationery Office.

CONTENTS

INTRODUCTION

'To tax and to please, no more than to love and be wise, is not given to men.
– Edmund Burke

I feel sure this phrase echoes the sentiments of most of my readers. Nevertheless, while we may all harbour a dislike for taxation, we do have a responsibility for paying the taxes which are legally due from us. The purpose of this book is twofold. Firstly, to help you understand your responsibilities as a taxpayer and deal with them in a proper manner. Secondly, while the book is not intended to be a comprehensive guide to every aspect of personal taxation, I hope it will also give you some ideas about how to reduce the amount of tax you pay each year.

This revised edition of the Guide incorporates the changes in legislation brought about by last year's Finance Act. The major proposals on taxation announced by the Chancellor of the Exchequer in his 1985 Budget Statement are mentioned in the supplement at the end of the book.

1

HOW THE TAX SYSTEM FUNCTIONS

Before we look at the different types of taxable income and the various allowances and reliefs you can claim, I thought it would be helpful to give you an outline of the functions of the Inland Revenue departments which operate our tax system. Overall authority for administering the legislation enacted by Government is vested in the Board of Inland Revenue. Although there are now many specialist departments within the Inland Revenue it is likely that your only direct contact with the Revenue will be through your Inspector and Collector of Taxes.

The Inspector of Taxes

It is your Inspector of Taxes who sends out a Tax Return for you to complete every year. If you are either employed or a pensioner you can expect to receive this Return from the Inspector of Taxes who deals with the Pay-As-You-Earn affairs of your employer or his pension fund. It is not unusual for an employee's tax office to be many miles away from his home. For example, if you work in London your Inspector of Taxes is probably somewhere in Lancashire, Yorkshire or the West Country. Where you are self-employed you will find that your local tax office handles your Tax Returns.

Not only is your Inspector of Taxes responsible for sending you a Tax Return to complete but you can also expect to receive notices of coding, assessments and general correspondence on your affairs from the same office. A notice of coding tells you what allowances and reliefs are due to you, so indicating that part of your salary which is tax-free (see Chapter 4). An assessment is a calculation of the tax payable on a particular sort of income after deduction of any allowances or reliefs which are due to you.

The Collector of Taxes

The only responsibility of the Collector of Taxes, as the name implies, is to collect the tax which is due from you. Whenever your Inspector of Taxes sends an assessment to you the Collector is notified of the tax payable. If it is not paid by the due date you can expect to receive further demands until payment is made. Should you still fail to make payment the Collector will eventually institute proceedings for recovery of the tax by distraint.

If you are late in paying your tax and incur an interest charge it is the Collector who sends you a demand for the interest.

You can provide for the payment of a future tax liability by purchasing a Certificate of Tax Deposit. Certificates can be bought from the Collector of Taxes. They earn interest from the date of purchase up until the normal due date for payment of the liability (see Chapter 12). The interest is taxable.

Communicating with the Inland Revenue

On any straightforward matter where it helps you to have a quick answer it is better to telephone your tax office. Unless you specifically ask to speak to the Inspector you will be put through to one of his assistants who will usually be able to answer your enquiry. On a more involved aspect of your tax affairs I suggest you write to the tax office. Always remember to quote your reference number in any correspondence. Unfortunately, you may sometimes have difficulty in understanding the reply to your letter. I hope that by the time you have read this book you will be in a better position to decipher any correspondence, which at first sight looks horribly complicated. There are, of course, occasions when an exchange of letters will be initiated by your tax office. Where this happens, try to reply promptly and give the information requested in a clear and concise manner.

There may be times when a particular matter concerning your tax affairs can best be resolved by a detailed discussion. Then is the time to arrange a visit to your tax office. Where this is situated a long way from your place of employment or home you can always arrange to go to the nearest PAYE Enquiry Office. Remember that the Inspector of Taxes and his assistants are not responsible for making the legislation in our tax system. If you think you are being unfairly treated by the law there is no point in adopting an aggressive attitude at the interview. You will usually get a helpful response, especially if you adopt a polite approach to the Inspector or his assistant.

Where the Inspector has reason to believe that there has either been an omission of income from your Returns or an under-declaration of business profits he will often request a formal interview. At such a meeting the Inspector can be expected to pursue a wide-ranging line of questioning about your business activities and spending habits. You may well find some of the questions unreasonable or objectionable but it is one of the Inspector's duties to detect tax evasion and collect the tax due on the undeclared income. In the circumstances, the Inspector's line of questioning will probably be justified.

Changes in legislation

Every year, usually around Easter, the Chancellor of the Exchequer makes his annual Budget Statement. Not only does the Chancellor choose the occasion to introduce new or amending legislation to our tax laws, but he also announces the rates of tax and allowances for the following tax year.

The changes in legislation necessary to implement the Chancellor's proposals are subsequently published in a Finance Bill. The clauses in the Bill are debated and amendments are proposed to some of them. Subsequently, the Bill is passed by both Houses of Parliament and receives the Royal Assent. It is then republished as a Finance Act.

It is the fiscal legislation passed by Parliament which is administered by the Inland Revenue. On occasions when the law is either unclear or ambiguous the Inland Revenue publish a Statement of Practice showing how they intend to interpret it. There are also times when the Inland Revenue do not seek to apply the strict letter of the law. These are published as a list of Extra-Statutory Concessions.

The Inland Revenue also publish a number of booklets on different aspects of our tax system. A list of the most helpful booklets is set out in Table 2 at the end of the book.

Income Tax rates for 1984/85

Under our tax system, the tax (or fiscal) year runs from each 6 April to the following 5 April.

The rates of tax applying to all taxable income for 1984/85 are:

Band of Taxable Income £	*Rate of Tax* %	*Tax on Band* £	*Cumulative Tax* £
0–15,400	30	4,620	4,620
15,401–18,200	40	1,120	5,740
18,201–23,100	45	2,205	7,945
23,101–30,600	50	3,750	11,695
30,601–38,100	55	4,125	15,820
Over 38,100	60		

The law now provides that both the band of income taxable at the basic rate of 30% and the other rate bands are to be increased each tax year in line with the movement in the Retail Prices Index during the previous calendar year. As with the main personal allowances the Treasury can, however, order an increase different to the statutory commitment, providing Parliament agrees.

In previous years your investment income which exceeded a specified limit was also liable to a 15% surcharge. This has been abolished with effect from 1984/85.

2

PERSONAL ALLOWANCES AND RELIEFS

The rates of the various personal allowances for 1984/85 are:

		£
Personal allowance	– single	2,005
	– married	3,155
Wife's earned income relief		2,005
Age allowance	– single	2,490
	– married	3,955
Additional personal allowance		1,150
Widow's bereavement allowance		1,150
Housekeeper relief		100
Son's or daughter's services		55
Dependent relative relief		100 or 145
Blind person's relief		360

There is a section in your Tax Return for you to claim the particular allowances to which you are entitled. They are deducted from your total income to give the amount on which you are liable to pay Income Tax each year.

It is usual for the rates of allowances to vary from year to year. This is particularly so now since the law provides that the rates of the allowances set out above, with the exception of the last four, are to go up at the beginning of each tax year in line with the increase in the Retail Prices Index during the previous calendar year. The Treasury can, however, order an increase different to the statutory commitment providing Parliament agrees. For 1984/85 the amounts of those allowances which are subject to indexation, apart from the two age allowances, went up by over 12%. This was some 7% above the increase in the Retail Prices Index during 1983.

Personal allowances

If you are single, widowed, or your marriage has broken up you are entitled to the single personal allowance.

You will be due the higher married allowance if you are a married man whose wife is living with you. If you were married during the tax year the amount of your personal allowance depends upon when during the tax year the marriage took place. For every complete month from 6 April 1984 up to the date of your wedding the amount of your allowance is calculated by deducting from the value of the married allowance one twelfth of £1,150, that being the difference between the single and married allowances.

Illustration

A man who married on 16 July 1984 receives an allowance of £2,868 for 1984/85 as follows:

Married allowance	3,155
Less: Reduction	
3/12 × £1,150	287
1984/85 Allowance	£2,868

Wife's earned income relief

If you have a working wife she will benefit from being able to set this relief against her earnings. For this purpose earned income includes any pension she may be drawing from either the State or a previous employer's pension fund based on her own past contributions.

Age allowance

A pensioner whose income does not exceed a specified limit is entitled to a higher rate of personal allowance: this is known as the age allowance. It is due to a single person who is over age 65 during part or all of the tax year. For a married couple to benefit from this higher allowance it is only necessary for one of them to be at least 65 years old during part or all of the tax year.

As the age allowance is designed to help those pensioners who are less well off, it reduces where their income rises above £8,100 for 1984/85. The reduction in the age allowance is two thirds of the amount by which total income exceeds the stated limit of £8,100, although it cannot take the rate of the allowance below the level of either the single or married allowance as the case may be.

Illustration

An elderly married couple whose joint income amounted to £8,700 during 1984/85 are entitled to an allowance of £3,555, as follows:

Income before tax	£
State pension	2,890
Pension from former employer	3,800
Investment income	2,010
	8,700
Less: Income limit for age allowance	8,100
Excess	£600
Age allowance	3,955
Less: Reduction – 2/3 × £600	400
1984/85 Allowance	£3,555

The income limit for age allowance goes up each tax year in the same way as the main personal allowances.

Additional personal allowance

To qualify for this allowance you must be a person, such as a widow or widower, who is not entitled to claim the married allowance, or a married man whose wife is either physically incapacitated or mentally infirm. In either event you must have at least one child living with you who fulfils certain conditions. If the child is your own he or she must be under 16 at the start of the tax year. If older, he or she must still be at school or attending a full-time course at a university, college or similar place of education, including a training course for at least two years with an employer in some trade or profession. Where the child living with you is not your own then he or she must be under 18 years old at the beginning of the tax year and looked after at your own expense.

No matter how many children you may have living with you who fulfil these tests only one allowance can be claimed. If more than one person is in a position to claim the allowance for the same child then it will be apportioned between them.

Widow's bereavement allowance

Providing her husband was entitled to the married man's allowance at the time of his death, a widow can claim this allowance for both the tax year in which her husband dies and the following tax year as long as she has not remarried by the beginning of that year. As a wife who loses her husband during a tax year then becomes taxable as a single person, the bereavement allowance for that year is given as a deduction against her income from that moment onwards until the end of the tax year. For the following tax year this allowance is set against her total income.

Housekeeper relief

A widow or widower can claim this relief if he or she has a relative or a paid help living in as a housekeeper. If the housekeeper is a relative who is married, the opportunity for claiming this allowance is lost where the relative or her husband is receiving the married allowance. Furthermore, the housekeeper relief cannot be claimed if you are claiming the additional personal allowance.

Son's or daughter's services

A person who is elderly or sick enough to be forced to depend upon the services of a son or daughter can claim this relief. The son or daughter must live in and be supported by the claimant.

Dependent relative relief

This is an allowance for a person who helps towards supporting his own or his wife's dependent relative. The relative must be either a pensioner or too unwell to look after himself or herself, unless the relative is the claimant's mother or mother-in-law when it is sufficient if she is either widowed, separated or divorced. The higher allowance of £145 is given to a woman not living with her husband for each dependent relative for whom she can claim.

Where two or more people are in a position to claim for the same relative the allowance is apportioned between them. If the dependent relative's income exceeds the amount of the basic National Insurance Pension for a tax year the rate of allowance is reduced by the amount of the excess. The effect of this restriction is often to remove the ability to make a claim for this relief.

Blind person's relief

This relief is given to a registered blind person. If both husband and wife are blind they may each claim the relief. A blind person who could also claim the relief for the services of a son or daughter should forego that allowance as otherwise the blind person's relief will not be given.

Relief on life assurance premiums

These days life assurance serves many purposes. They range from providing for the payment of lump sums on death to either pay off the amount of an outstanding mortgage or leave a lump sum for the deceased's dependents, to other uses which can often serve as tax-efficient forms of investment.

The amount of tax relief on life assurance premiums is at the fixed rate of 15% on policies taken out before 14 March 1984. It should not be necessary for you to claim this since the premiums paid to the life assurance company are after deduction of the 15% tax relief. There are occasions when some or all of this relief can be withdrawn, and then a payment to the Inland Revenue will have to be made for the tax relief which has been lost. For example, the amount of premiums which can be paid in any tax year without restriction of the tax relief is limited to £1,500 or one sixth of your total income, before allowances, whichever is greater.

Illustration

A couple pay annual life assurance premiums of £1,700 before tax relief. If their income is:

(a) £12,000, the 15% tax relief is unrestricted;

(b) £8,000, they will only receive the 15% tax relief on premiums of £1,500.

Premiums payable on a life assurance policy taken out after 13 March 1984 do not attract any tax relief. The same applies to future premiums payable on a policy taken out before that date if, after 13 March 1984, the benefits secured under the policy are varied or its term extended.

Tax saver

One life assurance contract which currently features in ever-growing numbers in the financial press is that of a policy with a tax-exempt Friendly Society. The valuable attraction of a Friendly Society over a life assurance company is that it can write life policies under which the premiums are invested in a totally tax-exempt 'underlying fund'. As there is a restriction on the size of the benefits which may be secured under a tax-exempt Friendly Society policy there is a limit of just about £100 per annum on the amount of the annual premium that may be paid.

You qualify to take out this type of policy if you are married or single with dependent children. A husband and wife can each take out a policy in favour of the other.

As the opportunities for investing in a tax-free fund are limited you may well wish to consider this type of plan.

3

INTEREST PAYMENTS AND OTHER OUTGOINGS

As the opportunities to claim tax relief for interest paid on borrowed money are limited, you should be aware of the few occasions when you can do so. It is important to appreciate that the purpose for which a loan is raised governs whether the interest on it will be eligible for tax relief. How the loan is secured is irrelevant.

Generally the interest on which tax relief is due is deducted from your total income in the year of payment. This general rule does not apply where you borrow money to buy a property which you let out: this is dealt with later on in the chapter.

Your own home

If you have borrowed money from a building society, a bank or some other source to help you buy your home you will receive tax relief on the interest you pay each year. Your home can be a house or a flat; it may even be a houseboat or a caravan. For this purpose a caravan must be at least 22 ft long and 7 ft 6 in wide or permanently situated so that it is liable to local authority rates.

It is not only the purchase price of your home which governs the maximum amount of the loan on which interest qualifies for tax relief. The incidental costs of buying your home such as surveyor's and solicitor's fees and stamp duty all count as part of the cost price.

From time to time you may improve your home by perhaps either extending it or installing double glazing. If you meet this type of expenditure by either increasing your mortgage or taking a loan from your bank the interest will qualify for tax relief. The Inland Revenue has issued a list of most, but not all, of the types of expenditure on property improvements qualifying for tax relief. It consists of:

(a) Home extensions and loft conversions.
(b) Central heating installations (excluding portable radiators and night storage heaters).
(c) The installation of double glazing, even though it may be in a detachable form.
(d) The insulation of a roof or walls.
(e) Installation of bathrooms and other plumbing.
(f) Kitchen units, e.g. sink units, which are affixed to and become part of the building; in practice, a range of matching units, only some of which qualify, may be treated as qualifying as a whole (other than cookers, refrigerators and similar appliances).
(g) Connection to main drainage.
(h) Garages, garden sheds, greenhouses.
(j) The construction or landscaping of gardens.
(k) Swimming pools.
(l) Reconstruction of property, e.g. conversion into flats.

There is an overall limit on the amount of your loans for the purchase and improvement of your home above which the interest is no longer deductible from your income: for 1984/85 this limit is £30,000.

Illustration

Year	*Expenditure*		*Amount Borrowed*	*Interest Paid*
1978	House purchase	40,000		
	Professional fees and stamp duty	1,600		
		£41,600	£24,000 at 11% p.a.	2,640
1980	Double glazing installed	£3,000	£2,500 at 15% p.a.	375
1982	House extended	£8,000	£6,000 at 13% p.a.	780

Since the 1982 loan of £6,000 took the total borrowings above £30,000, not all the interest paid in 1984/85 on this latest loan will qualify for tax relief:

Interest paid: on 1978 and 1980 loans of £26,500		3,015
on 1982 loan: $\frac{3{,}500}{6{,}000} \times £780$		455
1984/85 Relief for interest paid		£3,470

If you are employed in some capacity that requires you to live in accommodation provided by your employer you can still in certain specific circumstances obtain mortgage interest relief on a loan to buy your own home. This also applies if you are self-employed and the terms of your trade or profession are such that you must live in accommodation provided for your use.

Most people move home at some time during their lifetime. It is often impossible to arrange for the sale of your present home to coincide with the purchase of your new one. To overcome such difficulties it is usual to arrange a short-term bridging loan. For a period up to a maximum of one year, interest payable on both the existing mortgage and the bridging loan will both qualify for tax relief, subject of course to the overall limitation of £30,000 on each loan.

Most of you are making your regular mortgage repayments after deduction of tax at the basic rate on the interest element in each repayment. This procedure is known as 'Mortgage Interest Relief at Source' – MIRAS for short. You do not have to pay this tax over to the Inland Revenue. This applies even where you have no taxable income, or where your income is less than your personal allowances. If your mortgage exceeds the limitation of £30,000 on which interest qualifies for tax relief you will receive relief on that part of the total interest payable equivalent to this limit. This relief is obtained either through the new tax deduction scheme or, as previously, through your PAYE coding. Only tax at the basic rate is taken off the interest at the time of payment, but despite that you are not denied relief at the higher rates of tax. This will still be given to you where your top rate of Income Tax is in excess of the basic rate.

A second home

If you can afford to run two homes – such as a house or flat in town for use during the weekdays and a cottage in the country for weekends – you will nevertheless only be able to claim tax relief on a loan to buy one of them. This will be granted on the mortgage interest to buy whichever of your homes is the main one. You cannot decide this for yourself. It is a matter of fact.

Alternatively, you may want to provide a flat or cottage for an elderly relative to live in. If you borrow money to help purchase a suitable home the interest on the loan will qualify for tax relief as long as the total amount of any borrowing for this purpose together with any outstanding mortgage on your own home does not exceed the overall limitation of £30,000. Where the amount of an additional loan lifts your borrowings above this threshold the interest on which tax relief will be given is proportionally reduced as already illustrated in this chapter.

The relative must be either a pensioner or too unwell to look after himself or herself, unless the relative is the claimant's mother or mother-in-law, when it is sufficient if she is either widowed, separated or divorced.

Let property

Interest on a loan taken out to buy or improve a property which you rent out is tax deductible. The interest is set against the rental income from the property. Should the interest payable in a tax year exceed the rents receivable in the same year, the excess can only be carried forward to future years.

Illustration

A property was bought in 1981 with the assistance of a £35,000 loan. It is let and the rents less expenses came to £4,000 and £6,000 during 1983/84 and 1984/85 respectively.

	1983/84 £		1984/85 £
Rents less expenses	4,000		6,000
Less: Loan interest paid	4,900	4,200	
Deficit carried forward	£900	900	
			5,100
1984/85 Taxable Income			£900

The property must be let at a commercial rent for at least 26 weeks in any period of 52 weeks. When it is not let it must either be available for letting or be undergoing repairs or renovations.

Business loans

Most businesses need to borrow money at some time for one purpose or another. Interest on any such borrowings is allowable as a deduction against your business profits providing the borrowed money is used for business purposes. It does not matter for this purpose whether the borrowings arise because your bank account goes overdrawn, or because you take out a loan for some specific purpose connected with your business.

If you need to borrow to buy an asset – such as a car or a piece of machinery – for use in your business, the interest you pay will qualify for tax relief but will be restricted where the asset is also used privately.

If you are about to become a member of a partnership, you may need to borrow money to purchase a share in the partnership or to contribute capital for use in its business. If that is the case, the interest on the borrowings will qualify for tax relief.

Alternatively, you may have business connections with a private company. The interest on a loan raised so you can either acquire shares in the company or lend it money for use in its business will qualify for tax relief. You must either own at least 5% of the company's share capital or have at least some shareholding and work for the greater part of your time in the business.

Employees who need to borrow to buy shares in their company as part of an employee buy-out are allowed tax relief on the interest.

Replacement loans

There are occasions when you might want to take out a fresh loan in order to repay an existing borrowing. If the interest on the mortgage or loan which is being replaced qualifies for tax relief then the interest on the replacement loan will also qualify for tax relief in the same way.

Deeds of covenant

Later on in this book (Chapter 8) we shall see how useful deeds of covenant can be when they are taken out in favour of children. They are also an effective way of making a donation to a charity. To be valid for tax purposes a deed must be capable of providing for regular annual payments over a minimum period of seven years, except where it is for the benefit of a charity. Then it is sufficient if a deed can exceed a period of only three years. The payer must deduct Income Tax at the basic rate from every payment under a deed. The tax deducted can be retained providing the payer has suffered tax at the basic rate which is at least equivalent to the tax deducted from all covenanted payments during a tax year.

It is the ability of the recipient to recover the Income Tax deducted which will often persuade the payer to take out a deed of covenant. This will always apply where charities are involved as they are exempt from tax on their income. As an incentive to individuals with high incomes they are allowed to deduct covenanted payments to charities up to £5,000 per annum gross each year from their income in calculating their higher-rate tax liabilities.

Alimony and maintenance payments

Where a marriage breaks down the husband will usually have to make payments to his former or separated wife under either a court order or a separation agreement. Income Tax at the basic rate must be deducted from these payments. Sometimes a court order can require that payments be made to the couple's children for their education and maintenance. These should also be made under deduction of tax unless they qualify as small maintenance payments. This is dealt with more fully in Chapter 7.

4

EARNINGS FROM EMPLOYMENT

Most of you will be familiar with at least some part or other of the Pay As You Earn (PAYE) system. It provides a mechanism for collecting the tax due on the earnings of those people in employment. Employers must deduct Income Tax from the earnings of their employees and every month the total of these deductions has to be paid over to the Inland Revenue. The PAYE taken off an employee's earnings is treated as a credit against the overall amount of tax payable by the employee for the tax year in question. In working out the amount of tax to deduct from each employee's salary or pay packet, the employer takes into account each individual's own allowances and other reliefs. This is possible because the Inland Revenue issue employers with a code number for each employee. In turn the code number incorporates each employee's allowances and reliefs. The system allows for these to be spread evenly throughout the tax year to avoid any substantial variation in the amount of tax deducted from each salary cheque or pay packet.

The sort of earnings which count as taxable income from an employment are:

An annual salary or wage
Overtime
Commission
Tips or gratuities
Holiday pay
Sick pay
Earnings from a part-time employment
Directors' fees or other remuneration
Benefits-in-kind

Code numbers

I have already mentioned that each employee is issued with a code number by the tax office. In theory the code number should ensure that the correct amount of tax has been deducted from your earnings by the end of the tax year. The system can only work properly and effectively if your local tax office is kept informed of any changes in your personal circumstances which affect the amount of your allowances or reliefs. For example, most if not all notices of coding for the 1985/86 tax year commencing on 6 April 1985 were issued during the early part of the year. This was before people came to complete their 1985/86 Income Tax Returns. The Return requires a report of each person's income for the tax year just finished – the year to 5 April 1985 – but the claim for allowances is for the following year – the year to 5 April 1986. It follows that the information on which all the code numbers for 1985/86 have been based is that of the previous year. This is why it is important you should check your code number for 1985/86 and write to your tax office setting out any alterations that are required to your allowances or reliefs. If the rate of any allowance has been altered in the Budget there is no need for you to communicate with your tax office – your employer will automatically have been instructed by the Inland Revenue about how to deal with this.

On the following page is an illustration of a notice of coding for 1985/86. It shows the taxpayer is a married man claiming relief for a dependent relative. His personal allowances for 1985/86 are £3,255 before deductions. The first three of these relate to benefits-in-kind in the form of a company car and private medical insurance cover provided by the taxpayer's employer. Some of the types of taxable expenses and benefits are dealt with later on in the chapter. The coding notice illustrates how the tax payable on benefits-in-kind is usually collected. This is done by restricting the taxpayer's allowances by the value of the benefits-in-kind. In the illustration they come to £1,200 reducing the allowances to £2,055. The final deduction is for tax underpaid for 1983/84 of £84. For any one of a number of reasons the allowances given in the coding notice may subsequently turn out to differ from

SPECIMEN FORM

How your PAYE code is calculated

Expenses		
Death and Superannuation Benefits		
Interest payable		
Personal allowance		3155
Age allowance (estimated total income £............)		
Wife's earned income allowance		
Additional personal allowance		
Dependent relative allowance		100
Widow's bereavement allowance...		
....		
....		
Total allowances		3255
Less allowances given against other income		
Untaxed interest...		
Occupational pensions		
Social security benefits		
CAR BENEFIT	525	
CAR FUEL BENEFIT	525	
MEDICAL INSURANCE	150	1200
Net allowances		2055
Less adjustments for		
....		
....		
Tax unpaid for earlier years 1983-84 £ 84.00	280	
equivalent to a deduction of		
198 -8 (estimated £....................)		
equivalent to a deduction of		280
Allowances given against pay etc.		1775

those actually due to the taxpayer. If, as a result, there is an underpayment of tax this is often collected in a later year, again by restricting the allowances in the coding. In our illustration a reduction in allowances for 1985/86 of £280 will result in the Inland Revenue collecting the underpayment of £84 (£280 at 30%) from the taxpayer during the year.

The combined effect of these adjustments is to leave the taxpayer with allowances of only £1,775 to be set against his salary for 1985/86. His code number will be 177H. Clearly, there is a direct link between the taxpayer's allowances and his code number. The suffix letter is added to the coding so that whenever there is a change in the rates of personal allowances it can be automatically implemented by the employer. The letter H indicates the taxpayer is entitled to the married man's personal allowance. A coding which includes the single personal allowance or the wife's earned income relief ends up with the letter L. For personal reasons you may not want your employer to know which personal allowance you are claiming. You should then ask for the suffix letter T to be included in your coding. Your employer must then wait for instructions from the tax office before making any changes to the coding. Where you have more than one employment you will probably find that all your allowances are given in calculating the PAYE due from your main employment. Your earnings from a subsidiary employment are likely to attract a coding prefixed by either the letter D or BR. A 'D' coding results in tax being deducted at one of the higher rates whereas 'BR' instructs the employer to deduct tax at the basic rate.

The assessment

Shortly after the end of each tax year every employer sends in to the Inland Revenue a Return summarizing the names of all employees, their earnings during the tax year, and the Income Tax deducted from them. At the same time the employer hands out a Form P60 to every employee. This is a certificate of the employee's earnings for the past tax year and the Income Tax deducted from them. For most employees this corresponds with the tax due on their earnings. It is not then necessary for the Inland Revenue to issue an assessment. You can, however, always ask for one.

If you do receive an assessment it will show the earnings from all your employments during the past tax year together with the amounts of tax deducted by your employers. If you were provided with any benefits-in-kind, such as the use of a company car, the value of these will also be shown on the assessment as an addition to your salary or wages. This information is supplied to your tax office by your employer on a Form P11D. The types of benefit-in-kind which are taxable are dealt with later on in this chapter. In addition to detailing your earnings, the assessment will also show the allowances and reliefs you have been given. The final part is a calculation of the Income Tax due for the year. The tax deducted by your employer under PAYE is set against the liability to arrive at the overall position. An assessment which shows an overpayment is always a welcome sight. It will usually come to you with a cheque in repayment of the tax overpaid. Alternatively, the Inspector of Taxes might ask you to complete a formal claim to repayment before the Inland Revenue send you their cheque. If you have not paid enough tax you may be asked to send the Inland Revenue a cheque for the underpayment. Where it is not substantial the Inspector of Taxes will usually decide to collect it by restricting your allowances through an amendment to your notice of coding. We have already seen how this works. You should check the assessment as soon as possible after you receive it. If you want to dispute the income on which your tax has been calculated the Inland Revenue allow you only thirty days to write about this.

Expenses

The rules which allow you to claim tax relief on expenses relating to an employment are extremely restrictive. They dismiss the possibility of claiming tax relief on almost all types of expenses which are not ultimately borne by the employer. This is because the employee has to show that any expenditure is incurred 'wholly, exclusively and necessarily' while performing the duties of the employment. If the employer has not been prepared to foot the bill for the expenditure involved, then the Inland Revenue infer it was incurred more as a matter of choice than of necessity. Nevertheless, where you personally meet the cost of an annual subscription to a professional body, you should include details on your Tax Return as it is deductible from your income. The Inland Revenue and the Trade Unions have agreed flat rate allowances for the upkeep of tools and special clothing for most classes of industry. The rates for 1984/85 are set out in Table 3. As an alternative, the individual may claim a deduction for his actual expenses on these items.

Tax saver

Most expenses you incur in your job or employment are probably borne by your employer, who either reimburses you on an expense claim or pays for them direct. Employees (including full-time working directors who own 5% or under of the company's shares) earning less than £8,500 per annum including expenses are not taxed on most benefits or perks provided by their employers. Other directors and employees, whose total earnings, including expenses, exceed £8,500 per annum, are generally taxed on the actual value of any benefits obtained from their employments. If you fall within this category we have already seen that information about your expense payments and benefits-in-kind is supplied to your tax office annually on a Form P11D. It is down to you to justify that you are not to be taxed on them. This should not cause you any difficulties where the expenses, such as travelling and entertaining, have genuinely arisen during the performance of the duties of your employment. Luncheon Vouchers up to 15p per day are tax free for everyone, but remember that the cost of travelling between your home and the office is not allowable for tax purposes.

The value of some benefits provided for directors or higher-paid employees are, however, calculated differently:

(a) Company cars

Generally regarded as the most valuable benefit which can be provided to a director or higher-paid employee, it is measured according to a fixed scale. For cars with an original value up to £16,000 this is determined by their cubic capacity. For more luxurious cars the benefit is governed by price alone. The full scale of benefits is:

Original Market Value of Company Car	1984/85 Under 4 years old	1984/85 4 or more years old	1985/86 Under 4 years old	1985/86 4 or more years old
	£	£	£	£
Up to £16,000 (1984/85) or £17,500 (1985/86)				
1300 c.c. or less	375	250	410	275
1301 c.c. to 1800 c.c.	480	320	525	350
Over 1800 c.c.	750	500	825	550
£16,001 to £24,000 (1984/85)	1,100	740	–	–
£17,501 to £26,500 (1985/86)	–	–	1,200	800
Over £24,000 (1984/85)	1,725	1,150	–	–
Over £26,500 (1985/86)	–	–	1,900	1,270

Where the business usage in a tax year is more than 18,000 miles the scale benefit is halved. Where it is under 2,500 miles per annum it is increased to $1\frac{1}{2}$ times the amounts in the above table. This higher rate is also charged where a director or higher-paid employee has a second company car.

If it is the company's policy to meet the cost of petrol for private motoring there is an additional taxable benefit. Again it is based on predetermined fixed amounts dependent on the cubic capacity of the company car, as follows:

Cubic Capacity	1984/85	1985/86
	£	£
1300 c.c. or less	375	410
1301 c.c. to 1800 c.c.	480	525
Over 1800 c.c.	750	825

(b) Living accommodation

In some trades it is established practice for the employer to provide living accommodation. This can also be desirable where there is a security risk. In either sort of situation no tax liability will fall on the director or higher-paid employee.

In other circumstances the director or higher-paid employee is chargeable to Income Tax on the annual value of the property after deducting any rent paid for it. The annual value of a property for these purposes is broadly equivalent to the gross rateable value.

(c) Beneficial loans

Loans from an employer which are either interest free or where the interest charged by the employer is below a commercial rate can give rise to a taxable benefit on the director or higher-paid employee. The benefit is calculated by applying the Inland Revenue's official rate of interest to the loan. The benefit is reduced by any interest actually paid on the loan. Where the value of the benefit is less than £200 no charge to tax arises.

Share options

Tax saver

No liability to Income Tax is imposed on a director or employee who acquires or disposes of ordinary shares under his employer's Share Option Scheme. The gain is measured by the difference between the sale proceeds and the cost at the date the option is granted and is charged to Capital Gains Tax at the time of disposal.

A number of requirements must be met by both the employee and the employing company. These are, however, less onerous than those in earlier profit-sharing and savings-related schemes.

Working abroad

If you have to go abroad on business you can reduce your Income Tax providing you spend at least 30 qualifying days overseas in any tax year. A qualifying day is one where you are both away from the U.K. at midnight and during which you substantially devote your time to working or travelling overseas. If your business trip abroad takes you away from home for at least a week, the full period will qualify for this type of relief providing your time away is as a whole substantially devoted to your overseas work. This allows you some spare time to relax or do some sightseeing without prejudicing your tax position. If you accomplish the 30-day target you receive tax relief on 12½% of the earnings appropriate to the number of days abroad on business, as follows:

Illustration

A salesman spent 44 qualifying days abroad on business during 1984/85. His salary and benefits amounted to £17,500. The foreign earnings deduction is:

$$£17{,}500 \times 44/365 \times 12\tfrac{1}{2}\% = £264$$

Where your job takes you overseas for longer periods of absence then your tax treatment in the U.K. is on an even more favourable basis. Providing you can establish a consecutive period of at least 365 days working overseas the exemption from Income Tax on the earnings from that employment is increased to 100%. You are allowed intermittent visits to the U.K. in establishing a qualifying period of at least 365 days. These must not amount to more than 62 days, nor in building up the qualifying period must they come to more than one sixth of the period starting from the outset. If you work abroad for a complete tax year you will probably become non-resident. This is dealt with more fully in Chapter 9.

If part of your salary is earned from an overseas employer then 12½% of this salary is not taxed here. It is a requirement that all the duties of the overseas employment be performed wholly abroad.

Payments on termination of employment

It is now common practice for an employee to be paid a lump sum on the termination of an employment. If the right to receive the payment arose during the period of employment then it is taxable in full in the same way as other earnings. Otherwise the lump sum payment is either wholly or partly tax free. The occasions when the payments are free of tax are:

(1) Where the employment ceases because of the death, injury or disability of the employee.

(2) Where most of the employee's time was spent working overseas for the employer.

(3) Where the lump sum payment is under £25,000.

Where the amount of the lump sum payment is more than £25,000 only the part of it over this limit is taxable. Nevertheless, the tax due is reduced. By how much the tax is reduced depends on the size of the lump sum payment. The taxable amount is treated as your top slice of income and the Income Tax payable on it is worked out. The reduction in tax payable is calculated according to the following table:

Slice of Lump Sum Payment	*Relief from Tax*
First £25,000	Exempt
Next £25,000	Tax reduced by one half
Next £25,000	Tax reduced by one quarter
Excess over £75,000	Taxed in full

Illustration

An employee who lost his job last September was paid a lump sum of £35,000 on the termination of his employment. He is a married man and his earnings during 1984/85 were £19,000. The couple's investment income was £3,500 for the same year. The taxable part of the lump sum is £10,000.

	Tax Payable	
	Ignoring lump sum	*With lump sum*
	£	£
Income		
Earnings	19,000	19,000
Taxable part of lump sum	–	10,000
Investment income	3,500	3,500
	22,500	32,500
Less: Personal allowance	3,155	3,155
	£19,345	£29,345

Income tax thereon:		
First £15,400 at 30%	4,620.00	4,620.00
Next £2,800 at 40%	1,120.00	1,120.00
Next £1,145/4,900 at 45%	515.25	2,205.00
Next £6,245 at 50%	–	3,122.50
	£6,255.25	£11,067.50

Tax due on lump sum:
$\frac{1}{2}$ × (£11,067.50 – £6,255.25) = £2,406.12

As your employer will operate PAYE on the taxable amount of the lump sum payment you will probably be due a refund as it is likely that too much tax will be deducted.

Any statutory redundancy payment you receive, although exempt from tax itself, has to be counted in with any other lump sum payment from your employer in working out the tax due on the lump sum.

National Insurance

Although it is not within the scope of this book to go into National Insurance in detail I cannot pass on to the next chapter without mentioning it briefly. During recent years it has had an ever increasing impact on your salary cheque or pay packet. Although certain allowances and reliefs are deductible in calculating how much Income Tax you pay on your earnings, no similar rules apply for National Insurance purposes. The rate of contribution is applied to your gross earnings. The current rates and the earnings levels on which they are calculated are set out in Table 4 at the end of the book.

5

THE SELF-EMPLOYED

You cannot simply choose to be taxed on your earnings as a self-employed person. It is a matter of fact whether you are working on your own account or for someone else as an employee. You are *not* self-employed if you are running your business through a company. If you are employed but have some other freelance business activity as well, you will be taxed on these profits as a self-employed person.

The obligations imposed on the taxpayer who is self-employed are more onerous than those which apply to the employee. Proper records must be maintained of all business transactions. At the end of each financial year they are all brought together into an account of the income and expenditure of the business for the past twelve months. Whenever possible a balance sheet should be drawn up showing the assets and liabilities of the business at the year end. It is also better to operate your business through a separate bank account.

Value Added Tax

Unless the turnover of your business is under £18,700 per annum it must be registered with the Customs and Excise for the purposes of Value Added Tax. If your takings are not up to this level you will only need to register when they amount to more than £6,200 in the previous calendar quarter, unless you can demonstrate your total turnover for the year will still not exceed £18,700. If your business is currently registered but the turnover is falling, there are also limits when you can apply to the Customs and Excise for the registration to be cancelled.

When you need to register you should ask for Form VAT 1 – 'Value Added Tax – Application for Registration' – from your local Customs and Excise office. Soon after you have completed the form and sent it off you will receive your registration certificate and a selection of notices and leaflets. These are intended both to help you to understand the workings of the tax, and to assist you in complying with all the rules and regulations.

As a registered business you are required to charge VAT on all your taxable supplies. There are two rates: nil, and the standard rate of 15%. Some types of business, for example those relating to finance and education, are exempt from VAT. The turnover from these does not count towards the £18,700 registration limit, and VAT on expenditure incurred in these activities cannot be recovered.

Every three months you have to complete a Return – Form VAT 100 – of all the VAT charged on your supplies or services during the period. From this total is deducted the VAT you have incurred on business purchases and overhead expenses for the same period. Where the Return ends up showing an amount due to the Customs and Excise you should send it off with a cheque in settlement of the amount due. If the VAT suffered on your business expenditure exceeds the VAT charged on your sales, the Return will show you are entitled to a repayment. This will be sent direct to your bank by the Customs and Excise.

Every now and then a Customs and Excise officer will visit you to make sure that you are keeping proper records of your business transactions and correctly dealing with your quarterly Returns. You should keep all your invoices as evidence of the VAT suffered on purchases and other expenses.

If you are in the retail trade there are special schemes for calculating how much VAT you need to pay. There are also particular rules which apply to items such as second-hand goods, motor cars and business entertainment. It is outside the scope of this book to go into these and others in detail.

Accounts

You can choose the date to which you make up the accounts of your trade or business each year. For this reason it is unlikely that the first accounts will cover a full year's trading activities. Thereafter your accounts should continue to be made up to the same date every year although you can alter this where you can show good reason for a change.

Your accounts should be drawn up to show the profit or loss earned in the financial year. This is not usually the simple difference between the cash received and the cash paid out. For example, if you sell to some of your customers on credit there will inevitably be some unpaid invoices at the end of the financial year. Nevertheless, the amount of these outstanding invoices needs to come into your accounts as income for that period. Equally, where amounts are owing to your suppliers at the year-end these must be brought into the accounts as expenses incurred in the year. If your trade is one where you need to keep a stock of raw materials or finished goods, the value of that stock at the year-end must enter your accounts. It will usually be valued at cost or, in the case of redundant or old stock, at realizable value.

Make sure you include in your accounts all the expenses of running your business. If, for example, your wife helps you by taking telephone messages or acting as your part-time assistant or secretary pay her a proper wage for these services. What you pay her can count as an expense in your accounts. She can then set off her wife's earned income relief against her wages. If these are less than £1,768 a year there will be no tax or National Insurance to pay on them. There will be some items of expenditure, such as a car used both privately and in your business, when it will be difficult to differentiate precisely between the private and business elements of the expenditure. Where there is this overlap you should agree the proportion which relates to your business with the Inland Revenue. If you do your office work from home you can include as a deduction in your accounts a proportion of your home expenses, such as rates, light, heat and insurance. Remember that if part of your home is used exclusively for business purposes, then should you come to

Tax saver

sell your house the profit on sale attributable to that part will *not* be exempt from Capital Gains Tax.

Illustration

Jim White is a successful greengrocer who has just taken on a second shop. In addition to the normal High Street trade, he supplies some of the local hotels on credit. One of these has gone out of business and Jim lost £190.

During the year Jim spent £1,300 on fixtures and fittings – including cash registers – for his new shop. He also bought another van for £5,500, and was allowed £1,000 for his old van in part exchange. He uses the family car partly for business, and keeps his account books and deals with business correspondence at home.

Jim White – Greengrocer

Income and Expenditure Account for the year ended 31 May 1984

EXPENDITURE	£		INCOME	£
Stock of produce at 1/6/83	100		Cash received from customers	120,000
Purchases during the year	89,600		*Add:* Outstanding accounts at year-end	1,500
	89,700			121,500
Less: Stock of produce at 31/5/84	180	89,520	*Less:* Accounts outstanding at beginning of year	800
				120,700
Shop expenses:				
Rent & rates	3,190			
Light & heat	510			
Insurance	265			
Repairs to glass frontage	130			
Cleaning	250			
		4,345		
Staff wages		11,760		
Wages to wife as part-time shop assitant		1,400		

Car & van expenses:				
	Car	*Van*		
Tax & insurance	180	230		
Petrol & oil	360	460		
Repairs & servicing	120	–		
Parking	–	80		
	660	770		
Business proportions	25%	100%	935	
Use of home as office:				
Rates		480		
Light & heat		445		
Insurance		95		
		1,020		
Business proportion		1/6th	170	
Telephone:				
Shop		160		
Home (50%)		70		
			230	
Postage & stationery			80	
Advertising			290	
Subscription to local Chamber of Commerce			30	
Entertaining			90	
Legal expenses:				
Collection of bad debt		135		
Lease on new shop		460		
			595	
Bad debt			190	
Donations			15	
			109,650	
Profit for the year			11,050	
			£120,700	£120,700

Computation of profits

It does not follow that the profit shown by your business accounts is the same as the one on which you pay tax. This is because some items of expenditure are specifically not deductible in computing your taxable business profits. Two types of expenditure which come into this category are business entertainment, unless it relates to overseas customers, and expenditure on items of a capital, as opposed to revenue, nature.

Illustration

Although Jim White's accounts for the year to 31 May 1984 show a profit of £11,050, his taxable profits are £11,615, as follows:

		£
Profit as per accounts		11,050
Add Disallowable expenses:		
Legal expenses for new lease	460	
Entertainment	90	
Donations	15	
	—	565
Profit as adjusted for tax purposes		£11,615

Assessment of profits

Your tax assessment is based on the profits for the accounting year which ended in the preceding year of assessment. For example, the profits from Jim White's greengrocery business for the year to 31 May 1984 will be taxed in 1985/86. The tax will be payable in two equal instalments on 1 January and 1 July 1986.

Where a new trade or business is set up, the assessments for more than one tax year are governed by the results for the first period of trading.

Illustration

Had Jim White only started trading as a greengrocer on 1 June 1983 his results for the year to 31 May 1984 would have formed the basis of his assessment for the first three years, as follows:

1983/84	
Profits earned in year of assessment – 10/12ths×profits in year to 31 May 1984	£9,679
1984/85	
Profits of first year's trading – year to 31 May 1984	£11,615
1985/86	
Profits shown by accounts ending in the preceding year of assessment – year to 31 May 1984	£11,615

Where it is advantageous the taxpayer can elect that the assessments for both the second and third years, but not only one of them, be adjusted to the actual profits earned in those years.

Tax saver

If you ever set up in business choose carefully the date to mark the end of your accounting year. It can often afford an opportunity to minimize the Income Tax payable during the early stages of a new business. As a general guide select a date shortly after 5 April, such as the end of each April or May – Jim White chose the latter.

Where a business ceases to function, the assessment for the final year will be based on the profits from 6 April up to the date of cessation. The Inland Revenue has the option to adjust the assessments for the two years, but not only one of them, prior to the year in which cessation takes place. The assessments are revised to the actual profits earned in those years where this is to the Inland Revenue's advantage.

Capital allowances

Although you cannot deduct expenditure on items of a capital nature directly from your business profits, you do receive allowances for them. They are known as capital allowances. Generally, the total allowances due for a year of assessment are measured by the capital transactions of your business in the accounting year which forms the basis of the assessment.

The rate of first-year allowance is presently 75% for expenditure on machinery, equipment, motor vans, fixtures and fittings. Expenditure incurred before 13 March 1984 attracted a 100% first-year allowance; the rate reduces to 50% on expenditure incurred after 31 March 1985. Motor cars only qualify for a reduced allowance of 25% per annum commencing with year of purchase. Thereafter the annual allowance of 25% is calculated on the balance after deduction of previous allowances. For cars costing more than £8,000 there is a maximum allowance of £2,000 per annum.

A separate 'pool' of expenditure must be maintained for each of these different categories, as follows:

(1) Plant and equipment qualifying for the 75% first year allowance

(2) Cars costing up to £8,000

(3) Each car bought for over £8,000

(4) Each asset used for both personal and business use

Where an asset on which capital allowances have been given is sold, such as Jim White's old van, the proceeds of sale must come into the computation of capital allowances. This can sometimes lead to a further allowance where an asset is sold for less than its written-down value for tax purposes. Alternatively, if it fetches an amount greater than its written-down value this can often mean that part of the allowances already given need to be withdrawn. These adjustments are respectively referred to as balancing allowances and balancing charges.

Illustration

Jim White's claim to capital allowances for 1985/86 based on his capital expenditure in the year to 31 May 1984 is:

		Pool	Car with private use
		£	£
Written down values brought forward from 1984/85		1,100	4,400
Less: Sale proceeds of van		1,000	
		100	
Additions in the year:			
New van (purchased July 1983)		1,300	
Equipment (purchased April 1984)		5,500	
		6,900	
Allowances due:			
First year – 100% on £1,300	1,300		
– 75% on £5,500	4,125		
Writing down 25%	25		
		5,450	1,100
Carried forward to 1986/87		£1,450	£3,300
Summary of allowances:			
First year		5,425	
Writing down	1,125		
Less: 75% private use of car	825		
		300	
1985/86 Capital allowances		£5,725	

Stock relief

You are only entitled to this relief if your business is one where you have to carry stock or have unbilled work-in-progress. It has been withdrawn for periods of account beginning after 12 March 1984; stock relief due for the period of account straddling 12 March 1984 is worked out as if your year-end was on that date. You calculate the amount of your relief by applying the change in a single index during the period of account to the value of your stock-in-trade or work-in-progress at the end of the previous period. The index is designed to reflect changes in the average price level of a selective sample of stocks held by businesses. It is known as the All Stocks Index and is published monthly by the Department of Industry. The movement in the Index each month during 1984 (until it was withdrawn) is shown in Table 5 at the end of the book.

Stock relief is deducted from your profits for the tax year corresponding to the period of account for which the relief is due. The first £2,000 of stock or work-in-progress does not figure in calculating the relief.

Illustration

A trader makes up his accounts to each 30 June. His stock at 30 June 1983 was £7,850. The stock relief due for the year to 30 June 1984 is:

	£
Value of stock at 30 June 1983	7,850
Less: Non-qualifying part	2,000
	£5,850

Stock relief due for 1985/86:
£5,850×4.64% = £271

Unless you cease trading or the scale of your business activities becomes negligible when compared to the previous six years, you will not lose any of the stock relief given to you. However, if either of these situations does arise all the relief allowed in the assessments for the previous six years will be charged to tax in the final period. None of the stock relief you have been allowed is lost if your business ceased after 12 March 1984.

Losses

Most businesses cannot escape going through a bad spell at some stage in their existence. Where the results of the business for the year show a loss you will be able to claim tax relief on the loss as increased by the amount of any claim to capital allowances or stock relief. The overall loss is set against your other taxable income for the same year – which will include the profits from your business for the previous accounting year. Any unused part of the loss can then be set against your taxable income in the subsequent year. The balance of the loss which is left over must be carried forward to be set against the profits from the same business in later years.

There is a set procedure for setting off the loss. It must first of all reduce your other earned income for the year, then your unearned income, followed by your wife's earned income and finally her unearned income.

Loss relief must be claimed by sending an election to your tax office within two years after the end of the tax year in which it arises.

Illustration

A trader suffered a loss of £4,500 in his business for the year ended 31 March 1985. His claims to capital allowances and stock relief for the year are £2,400 and £850 respectively. His own and his wife's investment incomes for 1984/85 were £500 and £300 respectively.

In the previous year to 31 March 1984 the trader's taxable profits were £5,300.

The total business loss is:

	£
Trading loss	4,500
Capital allowances	2,400
Stock relief	850
	£7,750

This is set off as follows:

Profits for the year to 31 March 1984 – taxed in 1984/85	5,300
Investment income – husband	500
– wife	300
1984/85 Loss relief claim	£6,100

The unrelieved loss of £1,650 can either be set off against the couple's investment income in 1985/86 or carried forward against future profits from the same business in later years.

If the end of your financial year does not coincide with the tax year, the loss should be split on a time basis between the tax years into which it falls.

Illustration

A trader incurred a loss of £3,000 in his business in the year to 31 December 1984. This will be apportioned as follows:

1983/84: 3/12ths × £3,000	750
1984/85: 9/12ths × £3,000	2,250
	£3,000

Alternatively where the loss arises in an established business the Inland Revenue will usually allocate the loss to the tax year in which the financial year ends.

Tax saver There is an alternative form of loss relief available for new businesses. It allows losses incurred during the first four years of assessment to be set against your income in the three years prior to that in which the loss arises. Relief is first of all given against your income for the earliest year. For example, if you started out in business during 1984/85 and incur a loss in the first period of trading the proportion attributable to the tax year 1984/85 can be set off against your income in 1981/82, 1982/83 and 1983/84, starting with 1981/82.

Frequently it is necessary to incur expenditure on a new business venture before it starts to trade. Any such expenditure incurred within three years prior to the commencement of trade is treated as a separate loss sustained in the tax year in which trading began.

Retirement annuities

As a self-employed person you will still want to provide yourself with a pension on retirement. The premiums you pay are allowed as a deduction from your profits. The maximum amount you can contribute each year is expressed as a percentage of your profits depending on your age:

Year of birth	*Percentage limit of profits*
	%
1907	32½
1908 or 1909	29½
1910 or 1911	26½
1912 or 1913	24
1914 or 1915	21
1916 to 1933	20
after 1933	17½

Up to 5% of your profits every year can be paid into a policy providing for the payment of a lump sum to your dependants in the event of your death. The lump sum would be free of Capital Transfer Tax. Premiums paid into this sort of policy count as part of the maximum permissible limit set out above.

Where you do not pay premiums up to the maximum permissible amount in any year the short-fall can be carried forward for up to six years. Relief outstanding for earlier years is used up before that still available for later years. **Tax saver**

Illustration

A trader has been in business for many years. Since 1980/81 he has not been paying the maximum permissible premiums towards his pension, as follows:

Tax Year	*Premiums Paid*	*Maximum Permissible*	*Shortfall*
	£	£	£
1980/81	400	800	400
1981/82	450	840	390
1982/83	450	615	165
1983/84	500	735	235

During 1984/85 he paid premiums of £1,720; the maximum permissible premium limit for the year was £900. Nevertheless relief will be given for £1,720, as follows:

	£	£
Premium limit for 1984/85		900
Unused relief:		
1980/81	400	
1981/82	390	
1982/83 (part)	30	
	—	820
1984/85 Retirement annuity relief		£1,720

Premiums paid in the year can either be deducted from your taxable profits in the year of payment, or alternatively you can elect for them to be treated as if paid in the preceding year.

Although these policies are generally referred to as self-employed retirement annuities they can also be taken out by employees who are not members of their employer's pension scheme.

Working abroad

Where you spend more than 30 qualifying days abroad on business your taxable profits for that year of assessment are reduced. The definition of a qualifying day is similar to that which applies to an employee who has to go overseas on business. If you meet the 30-day target you receive tax relief on 12½% of your taxable profits appropriate to the number of days abroad on business, as follows:

Illustration

A trader spent 34 qualifying days abroad on business during 1984/85. His taxable profits after capital allowances and stock relief for the year ended 30 September 1983 were £11,000. The foreign earnings deduction for 1984/85 is:

$$£11{,}000 \times 34/365 \times 12\tfrac{1}{2}\% = £128$$

National Insurance

Like any employee you must pay National Insurance contributions if you are self-employed. There are two rates. Class 2 is a weekly flat rate and Class 4 is based on a percentage of your business profits. If your earnings are below a specified limit you can be excepted from payment of Class 2 contributions. Table 4 at the end of the book sets out the rates for both Classes during 1983/84 and 1984/85.

Special situations

In the space available it has only been possible for me to paint a general picture of the way in which business profits are taxed. If you are a farmer, writer or sub-contractor in the construction industry you should be aware that there are special rules which apply in calculating the tax on the profits from your trade or profession.

The letting of holiday accommodation in the U.K. is now treated as a trade. The accommodation has to be furnished residential property which is available for renting by the public as holiday accommodation for at least 140 days during each tax year. It must actually be let for a minimum of 70 days. There are other requirements which also need to be satisfied. Capital gains on disposals of holiday accommodation falling within these rules qualify for the replacement and retirement reliefs which apply to business assets (see Chapter 10).

There are also a number of specific rules which apply to the taxation of the profits of a partnership and in determining each individual partner's share of the partnership assessment. In these and other situations it is advisable to seek professional assistance in dealing with the tax affairs of the business concerned.

6

INVESTMENT INCOME

Most of you will at some time or other need to look into the various types of investment on offer. Perhaps you will be looking to find a suitable home for regular savings or to invest a more substantial amount such as an inheritance or a lump sum on retirement. As you no longer have to pay more tax on investment income it is now far less important to be able to distinguish it from earned income. Salaries, wages, directors' fees, business profits and pensions are examples of earned income. Investment or unearned income is that which does not depend on your active involvement or physical effort in some business or trade. Bank or building-society interest, dividends on shares or unit trust holdings, rents, income from a trust and interest on government stocks are all examples of investment income.

Investment income is subject to tax at both the basic and higher rates in the same way as earned income.

Tax-free income

The most widely known investments where the return is free of both Income Tax and Capital Gains Tax are some of those available from the Department for National Savings. They are:

Tax saver

- Fixed Interest and Index-linked Savings Certificates
- Yearly Savings Plan
- Premium Bond Prizes
- First £70 of annual interest on a National Savings Bank Ordinary Account

Apart from interest on any National Savings account, no details of these need to be shown on your annual Income Tax Return.

Rental income

If you own a flat, house, shop or some other property which you have let out to tenants you must show the rents and expenses on your Tax Return. The Income Tax payable on your net rental income is due on 1 January each year. For example, the tax payable for 1984/85 was due on 1 January 1985. You may well ask how the right amount of tax payable can be calculated when the exact amount of rental income is not known at the time. The answer is that the Inspector of Taxes issues a provisional assessment based on the agreed income for the previous year. This is adjusted when the current year's income is ascertained.

Apart from expenditure of a capital nature, such as that on structural alterations or improvements to a property, the general running costs of a property can be set against the rental income.

Illustration

	£	£
Rent receivable from letting a house		4,800
Less: Expenses		
General rates	500	
Water rates	70	
Building insurance	90	
Redecorating two bedrooms	300	
Repairs to door locks and drains	150	
Agents fees for collecting rent	165	
		1,275
1984/85 Net rental income		£3,525

If you are letting a furnished property you can claim an additional deduction to cover the cost of wear and tear to furnishings and fittings. This allowance is based on 10% of the rent less the amount of the general and water rates. If the property in the preceding illustration is let furnished this allowance would be £423, as follows:

Illustration

Rent receivable	4,800
Less: General and water rates	570
	£4,230
Wear and tear allowance: 10%	£423

The rules dealing with the taxation of premiums on leases and the situations where losses arise on the letting of properties are more complicated and outside the scope of this book.

Dividends and interest

The table below sets out the types of investment where the dividends and interest are paid to the investor after deduction of Income Tax at the basic rate, together with those where no such deduction is made.

Tax deducted at source
Dividends on shares and unit trust holdings
Building society interest
Interest on British government stocks

Not taxed at source
Bank deposit interest
Interest on National Savings income and deposit bonds
Interest on National Savings ordinary and investment accounts

Many people mistakenly assume – because the dividends and interest mentioned in the first table are paid after tax at the basic rate has been deducted – that they need not be reported on their annual Tax Return. This misunderstanding is most particularly associated with building society interest. Whatever the amount of your dividends and interest these details must be shown on your Tax Return. You may be entitled to a tax repayment or the size of this income may be such as to give rise to a liability to tax at the higher rates.

Always remember that you can never recover the notional tax deducted from building society interest. This can be of particular relevance to taxpayers living on low fixed incomes. Where their total income is below their personal allowances they will be able to recover any Income Tax paid providing none of their income comes from a building society.

Interest on the various accounts in the second table above is taxed in a special way similar to the income or profits from self-employment. Where an account has been in existence for at least three years the interest earned in a tax year is the amount on which tax is paid in the following year. However, there are special rules for determining the interest which is taxable – not only in the early years after a new account is opened, but also in the final years before one is closed.

Illustration

A bank deposit account was opened in November 1982. The interest received and amounts taxable are:

Interest received Date	Amount £		*Tax Year*	*Interest taxable* £	*Comments*
Dec 82	20		1982/83	20	Actual year's interest
Jun 83	105	£235	1983/84	235	Actual interest received in the year
Dec 83	130				
Jun 84	115	£205	1984/85	235	Interest received in the previous year
Dec 84	90				

The taxpayer can elect for the interest taxable in the third year – 1984/85 – to be adjusted to the actual interest received in the year. In the above illustration the taxpayer would exercise this option and the assessment would be reduced to £205. **Tax saver**

Where a more substantial amount of money is involved it can be deposited with a bank at a fixed rate of interest for a set period. This can vary from between one month to a year. Each deposit is looked at separately. The interest taxable each tax year will be the actual interest earned in it.

As with income from property, Income Tax on untaxed interest is payable on each 1 January.

Single premium bonds

Guaranteed income bonds and investment bonds offered by most insurance companies fall within this category. A lump sum premium is paid at the outset. The investor can usually either draw an income from the bond or leave it untouched until it is subsequently cashed in. No tax relief is due on the single premium. The proceeds of a single premium bond are not liable to Capital Gains Tax or Income Tax at the basic rate. There can be a liability to tax at the higher rates on the profit element, depending on the level of the investor's income in the tax year the bond is encashed. The method of calculating the additional Income Tax due on the gain from a single premium bond involves a number of stages.

Illustration

A married man invested £10,000 in a single premium bond in 1980. He cashed it in during 1984 for £16,000. His income for 1984/85 was £21,735, of which £12,235 was earned and £9,500 was investment income.

Gain on encashment of bond		£6,000
Number of years held		4
Taxable slice of gain		£1,500
Taxable Income		£
Earnings		12,235
Investment income		9,500
Slice of gain		1,500
		23,235
Less: Personal allowance		3,155
		£20,080
Tax payable thereon excluding slice of gain:		
First £15,400 at 30%		4,620
Next £2,800 at 40%		1,120
Next £380 at 45%		171
	£18,580	£5,911
Slice of gain of £1,500 will attract a tax rate of		45%

Therefore the rate of tax to apply to the gain is:
45% – 30% (basic rate) = 15%

The tax payable on the gain = £6,000 at 15% = £900

Forestry

Investing in woodlands on a commercial basis with a view to profit is likely to be of great interest to the high taxpayer. You can send an election to the Inland Revenue requiring your woodlands plantation to be taxed as if it were a business. This enables all the costs of planting, management and interest on money borrowed to finance the purchase of the land to be offset against your other income. Once you have made this election you can never switch back to the alternative basis of being taxed on just a nominal value representing the annual value of the land. Ideally, you would want to do this just before the woodlands mature and you come to sell the timber from the felled trees. To overcome this difficulty you can either sell the plantation or, for example, transfer the woodlands down to your children. If you do this the overall result is that the earlier losses on the planting and maintenance expenditure qualify for tax relief whereas the subsequent profits from the sale of the timber are tax free. **Tax saver**

Business Expansion Scheme

The concept of granting tax relief on minority investments in new companies was introduced in 1981 under the umbrella of the Business Start-Up Scheme. Commencing with the tax year 1983/84 changes have been made to the original scheme to make it more attractive to potential investors. Nevertheless there are still many conditions which must be met both by the individual and the company whose shares are being acquired. **Tax saver**

The scheme is now known as the Business Expansion Scheme. It is running for four years until 5 April 1987. The maximum amount that an individual may now invest in additional ordinary shares in new or established trading companies whose shares are not quoted on a recognized stock exchange is £40,000 per year. The minimum investment limit remains at £500. For husbands and wives these limits apply to them jointly. The relief is deductible from the investor's total income in the year in which the shares are issued. If they are disposed of within five years the relief can be reduced or withdrawn. Because of the numerous restrictions the most suitable way of taking advantage of this relief could be through one of the many special investment funds now formed for this purpose.

7

THE FAMILY UNIT

The concept of the family unit has long been the framework around which our tax system is built. Unless the married couple elect to be separately assessed, responsibility for completing the annual Tax Return rests with the husband. There are situations, such as a wife earning a salary subject to PAYE, when she pays the tax on her income. Otherwise it is the husband who has to pay the tax on the couple's joint income. However, if he fails to pay his tax the wife can then be asked to pay the tax due on her income.

Although children are part of the family unit they are treated as separate individuals for tax purposes. For this reason I have devoted a whole chapter (Chapter 8) to the position of children in our tax system.

Marriage

It is a general principle that the incomes of husband and wife be joined together to calculate the tax payable by the married couple. The first time this happens is the tax year following that in which they are married. For example, a couple whose wedding was in July 1984 will be taxed as single persons for 1984/85. Their incomes will first be aggregated in 1985/86.

Beginning with the year of marriage the husband is entitled to the married man's personal allowance. This was referred to in Chapter 2.

Separate assessment

Unlike the separate taxation of a wife's earnings there is no saving in tax from separate assessment. It is only helpful for the couple who wish to maintain some degree of privacy from one another in their financial affairs. The election to be separately assessed can be made by either husband or wife. It must be in writing and be made within the six months prior to 5 July in the tax year when it is intended to come into effect. For example, an election for separate assessment for 1985/86 must be sent to the Inland Revenue at any time in the six months up to 5 July 1985. Once it has been made, the election stays in operation until it is withdrawn within the same time limit.

Under a separate assessment election husband and wife each complete their own Tax Returns in the same way as if they were still single. They are also responsible for paying the tax due on their respective incomes. It is down to the Inland Revenue to work this out. After the two Tax Returns have been received the tax payable on the joint income is calculated and the total is apportioned between husband and wife in ratio to their income.

Illustration

	Joint	*Husband*	*Wife*
	£	£	£
Earned income	20,000	11,500	8,500
Investment income	3,000	2,500	500
	23,000	14,000	9,000
Less: Mortgage interest	2,000	2,000	–
Taxable income before allowances	£21,000	£12,000	£9,000
Income Tax thereon:	7,000		
Divisible:			
Husband $\frac{12,000}{21,000} \times 7,000$		4,000.00	
Wife $\frac{9,000}{21,000} \times 7,000$			3,000.00

Personal allowance	3,155					
Wife's earned income allowance	2,005					
Apportioned 4,000:3,000	£5,160		£2,949		£2,211	
Relief in terms of tax for personal allowances						
£2,800 at 45%	1,260		720.10		539.90	
£2,360 at 40%	944		539.51		404.49	
		2,204		1,259.61		944.39
1984/85 Tax payable under separate assessment		£4,796		£2,740.39		£2,055.61

The calculations can be even more involved when the couple's income comes from a number of sources and they are claiming various deductions and reliefs. Where the wife has earned income her share of the allowances must never drop below the allowance on this earned income.

Separate taxation of wife's earnings

Tax saver

A saving in tax can be achieved when a married couple make this election. Whether it benefits them depends on both the level of their joint income and the amount of the wife's earned income. This can be either a salary, profits from a business, or her own pension. What happens when an election is made is that the wife's earned income is separated from the couple's other income and is taxed separately. Their other income, including any income from the wife's investments, is still taxed on the husband.

The husband loses the married man's allowance and receives the single allowance instead. Before the husband and wife can benefit from making the election they must be able to reduce their tax payable at the higher rates by an amount at least equivalent to that on the loss of the married man's allowance.

The couple's allowances and reliefs are allocated in the same way as if they were still single persons. The relief for mortgage interest payments is given to the borrower. Where there is a joint mortgage the relief will be given to the spouse who makes the repayments to the bank or building society. When an election is in force it can sometimes be to the couple's advantage for the wife to pay part or all of the interest on a joint mortgage.

It is not possible to generalize on the income level needed before a saving in tax is achieved by making this election. Every couple should do their own calculations. Where the deductions from their income are confined to their personal allowances, their joint income must be at least £23,793 for 1984/85. The wife's earned income must come to more than £6,388, as must the husband's income from all sources, both earned and unearned.

Illustration

		Joint		*Separate*		
				Husband		Wife
		£		£		£
Earned income		27,000		20,000		7,000
Investment income						
Husband		2,500		2,500		
Wife		500		500		
		30,000		23,000		7,000
Less:						
Personal allowance	3,155		2,005			
Wife's earned income allowance	2,005				2,005	
Mortgage interest	2,000		2,000			
		7,160		4,005		2,005
Taxable income		£22,840		£18,995		£4,995
Income tax thereon						
at 30%	15,400	4,620	15,400	4,620.00	4,995	1,498.50
at 40%	2,800	1,120	2,800	1,120.00		
at 45%	4,640	2,088	795	357.75		
		£7,828		£6,097.75		£1,498.50
					£7,596.25	
1984/85 Saving in tax from a wife's earnings election						£231.75

An election for the separate taxation of a wife's earnings must be made jointly by both husband and wife. It can be made at any time in the period beginning six months before and ending twelve months after the tax year to which it relates. For example, for the tax year 1985/86 an election is valid if made between 6 October 1984 and 5 April 1987. Once an election has been made it applies every year until it is withdrawn. A couple should always review their situation each year as it does not follow they will benefit from it each year. An election can be withdrawn by a husband and wife acting jointly up to twelve months after the end of the tax year for which they no longer want it to apply.

Separation and divorce

Not only can the breakdown of a marriage cause much personal suffering, particularly when there are children of the marriage, but invariably it also calls for a reorganization of the parted couple's financial affairs. From the time they are permanently separated they are again taxable as single persons. When separation occurs midway through a tax year the wife is entitled to set the single allowances against whatever income she receives in the rest of the year. The husband's taxable income includes his wife's income up to the breakdown of the marriage. He still receives the married man's allowance for that year.

Tax saver

I referred in Chapter 2 to the additional personal allowance and the situations when it can be claimed. When a couple split up any children of the marriage usually go and live with their mother. She can claim the additional personal allowance. Nevertheless, where a couple have at least two children it should be possible for both their father and mother to benefit from the additional personal allowance. Each would claim for one of the children.

Whenever the husband pays maintenance to his former or separated wife under a court order he must deduct Income Tax at the basic rate from the payments unless they come within the limit of 'small maintenance payments'. Currently this is £33 per week or £143 per month. If the maintenance is payable under a private separation agreement he must always deduct tax from these payments.

The full amount of the maintenance payments made by the husband are deductible from his income in calculating the tax on it. In the hands of the wife they are taxable income from which tax at the basic rate has been deducted. Payments of maintenance or alimony are not treated as investment income. Depending on the overall level of her income the wife can expect either a refund from the Inland Revenue or an assessment to collect the additional tax due from her.

A court often orders payments to be made either direct to a child of the marriage or to another person, usually the mother, for the child's benefit. The present limits up to which payments for children can be made without deduction of tax at the basic rate are:

(1) Payments to a person under 21 years of age for his own benefit, maintenance or education: £33 per week or £143 per month

(2) Payments to any person for the benefit, maintenance or education of a person under 21 years of age: £18 per week or £78 per month

Tax saver

A considerable saving in tax can often be achieved by structuring the amount of maintenance payable by the husband in such a way that a proportion is paid to his children. They can then claim their personal allowance against the court order payments.

Illustration

A couple's marriage has broken down. The husband has agreed to pay his wife £8,000 per annum under a court order. Alternatively he could agree to reduce to £5,500 the amount paid to his wife, with the court order directing that payments of £1,250 per annum be made to each of the two children of the marriage.

Where the wife receives all the maintenance

		£
Payments under court order		8,000
Less: Personal allowance	2,005	
Additional personal allowance	1,150	
		3,155
Taxable Income		£4,845
Income Tax thereon at 30%		£1,453.50

Where the maintenance is split between wife and children

		Wife £	Child 1 £	Child 2 £
Payments under court order		5,500	1,250	1,250
Less: Personal allowance	2,005		2,005	2,005
Additional personal allowance	1,150			
		3,155		
		£2,345	Nil	Nil
Income Tax thereon at 30%		£703.50		

1984/85 Reduction in Income Tax payable £750

Old age

Unfortunately, the elderly taxpayer has to cope with the tax system in exactly the same way as the rest of us. Nevertheless, there are some factors which are only relevant in calculating the tax payable on the elderly person's income. The first of these is the age allowance. In Chapter 2 I explained how a pensioner calculates whether he or she is entitled to this allowance.

Apart from the war widow's pension, a pension from either the State or a past employer's pension fund is taxable.

A wife's pension based on her own past contributions attracts the wife's earned income relief. Although it is taxable, no tax is deducted at source from the National Insurance Pension. A pension from a former employer's pension scheme is taxed under PAYE. In addition to including the pensioner's personal allowances the coding notice will incorporate a deduction equivalent to the State retirement pension. In this way the tax due on it is collected. The necessity of a direct payment of tax is avoided.

Illustration

	£
Pension from former employer	3,900
National Insurance pension	2,890
	6,790
Less: Married age allowance	3,955
Taxable income	£2,835
Code number based on:	
Personal allowance	3,955
Less: State Pension	2,890
	£1,065

Code allocated: 106V

A code number ending with the letter V indicates the pensioner is entitled to the married age allowance. A coding which includes the single age allowance finishes up with the letter P. In the exceptional situation of the deduction for the State Retirement Pension exceeding the pensioner's personal allowances, the Inland Revenue issue an F coding. This is an instruction to apply a special rate of tax in calculating the deductions under PAYE on the pension from a previous employer's pension fund. Nevertheless, there will still be some circumstances where it is just not possible to collect all the tax due on the elderly taxpayer's pensions under PAYE. Then it is necessary for the tax office to issue an assessment. The tax payable will be due in four equal instalments.

When a person retires and starts to draw the old age pension, the Department of Health and Social Security send out a form to find out the tax office which deals with the pensioner's Tax Return. The purpose behind this is to enable the Department to tell the new pensioner's tax office of the amount of his or her National Insurance Pension and each subsequent increase. This will help make sure the correct deduction for the State pension is always included in the pensioner's code number.

If you have an elderly relative living on a low fixed income who you are helping to support you should consider doing this by way of a deed of covenant (see Chapter 3). Although it is outside the scope of this book, elderly people can often obtain rent or rate rebates or other benefits from the Department of Health and Social Security.

Death

Sadly, death comes to all of us sooner or later. Needless to say it also has some consequences so far as taxation is concerned. From the date of death the surviving spouse is again taxable as a single person. When death occurs midway through a tax year the widow is entitled to set her allowances against whatever income she receives in the rest of the year. In addition, she can claim the widow's bereavement allowance (see Chapter 2). In the year of death the husband is taxed on the couple's joint income up to the date of death. He does not lose his entitlement to the married man's allowance for that year.

If the wife dies first the husband can disclaim liability for any tax due on her income for the tax year in which death takes place. This will then have to be met by her executors out of her estate.

8

CHILDREN

Like you or I a child is a potential taxpayer so far as the various taxes on income and capital are concerned. The Income Tax liability of a minor child is calculated in exactly the same way as that for anyone else. A child is entitled to the single personal allowance. If he is married he can claim the higher married man's allowance. If all this tempts you to think about giving some of your savings to your children so that the Income Tax on the interest or dividends can be recovered by set-off against their personal allowances then I'm afraid I have to disappoint you. The income from a gift or covenant made by a parent in favour of an unmarried minor child is still regarded as the parent's income for tax purposes. Grandparents or other relatives can, however, transfer some of their income over to their grandchildren or nieces, nephews, etc. This is most commonly done under a deed of covenant, which is dealt with later on in this chapter. Responsibility for completing a minor's Income Tax Repayment Claim rests with a child's trustee or guardian.

A minor child is also a taxable person for the purposes of Capital Gains Tax (see Chapter 10) and Capital Transfer Tax (see Chapter 13).

Allowances and benefits

There is no longer any general tax allowance for children. You will probably be able to claim the additional personal allowance if you are single and have a child living with you (see Chapter 2).

The tax allowance for children was replaced by Child Benefit. Generally, this is payable to the mother. The present rate is £6.85 per week for each child. It is not taxable. Depending on your personal circumstances you may be entitled to one or more of the numerous other Social Security Benefits associated with children, but unfortunately it is outside the scope of this book to detail them.

Investment of savings

Most parents will usually opt for either a building society or bank deposit account when investing their child's savings. In the chapter on investment income (Chapter 6) I compared the payment of interest on a bank deposit account, where tax is not deducted at source, with that paid on a building society account. Here the interest is paid to the investor after deduction of Income Tax at the basic rate. This can never be recovered even if your child's income is beneath the level of his or her personal allowance. Accordingly you should compare the gross rate of interest on a bank deposit account with the net rate on a building society account when deciding which offers the best return for your child's savings.

The various types of National Savings can also be used for the investment of children's savings. An added attraction is their degree of security.

Deeds of covenant

These are by far the most common way of giving a child a tax free income up to the level of the single personal allowance. The general conditions which must be satisfied for a deed of covenant to be valid were set out in Chapter 3. There are two main occasions when a not insignificant saving in Income Tax can be achieved by executing a deed of covenant in favour of a child.

Tax saver

The first is when the child is still a minor. This is where the generous grandparent or other relation, except the parent, can help. The annual amount payable under the deed can be used by the parents for the general education and wellbeing of the child. This may be particularly helpful for parents whose children are being privately educated. Where the child is still a minor the covenant should be drawn up in favour of trustees, usually the parents, for the child's benefit.

Illustration

THIS DEED OF COVENANT is made the [*date of deed*] between [*name of person making covenant*] of [*address of person making covenant*] (herinafter called 'the Grantor') of the one part and [*name of first trustee*] of [*address of first trustee*] and [*name of second trustee*] of [*address of second trustee*] (hereinafter called 'the Trustees') of the other part.

THIS DEED WITNESSETH AS FOLLOWS:
1. The Grantor hereby covenants with the Trustees that the Grantor will pay to the Trustees on [*date of payment*] in each year for the period of seven years or the period of the joint lives of the Grantor and [*name of child beneficiary*] of [*address of child*] (hereinafter called 'the Beneficiary') whichever period shall be the shorter the gross sum of [*gross annual amount of covenant*] the first payment to be made on the [*the date of first payment*].

2. The Trustees shall hold the said sums upon trust for the Beneficiary absolutely.

3. The power of appointment of new or additional Trustees shall be vested in the Grantor during his/her lifetime.

IN WITNESS whereof the parties hereto have hereunto set their hands and seals the date and year first before written.

Signed Sealed and Delivered by
the said [*name of person making covenant*]
in the presence of:
[*name and address of witness*]
[*signature of person making convenant*] [*seal*]

Signed Sealed and Delivered by
the said [*name of first trustee*]
in the presence of:
[*name and address of witness*]
[*signature of first trustee*] [*seal*]

Signed Sealed and Delivered by
the said [*name of second trustee*]
in the presence of:
[*name and address of witness*]
[*signature of second trustee*] [*seal*]

Where, for example, the gross amount covenanted by a

grandparent is £1,500 he or she deducts Income Tax at 30% of £450 for each annual payment to the child's trustees. They receive £1,050 from the grandparent and the remaining £450 from the Inland Revenue. To give the child £1,500 only costs the grandparent £1,050.

Illustration

	Income	*Tax*
	£	£
Annual payment under deed of covenant	1,500	450
Less: Personal allowance	2,005	
Taxable income	Nil	Nil
Tax repayable		£450

Providing the grandparent has sufficient income each year taxable at the basic rate to cover the gross amount payable under the covenant, his or her Income Tax position should be unaffected. In view of the various exemptions set out in Chapter 13 a charge to Capital Transfer Tax on the amount of the covenant is unlikely to arise.

The second and more popular use of a deed of covenant is that taken out by a parent in favour of a child of his or hers who is either over 18 or married and still in full-time education. This type of covenant is commonly known as a student deed of covenant. As a covenant must be capable of exceeding a period of six years to be valid for tax purposes, this condition must still be included in the deed. However, as the deed is really only intended to cover the period until the adult student ceases full-time education this additional factor also needs to be mentioned. Even though a period of further education at a university or college is unlikely to last for more than four years, it is conceivable that it could go on for longer and, therefore, the extra wording does not invalidate the deed. It will frequently be attractive for the annual amount under a deed to be payable in instalments to coincide, for example, with the beginning of each term at college or university. As a help to parents the Inland Revenue has issued an acceptable form of wording for a deed of covenant by a parent to an adult student. This is contained in Form IR47. In addition to setting out the procedure to be followed and the points to note the form contains a specimen deed of covenant, as follows:

Illustration

To be completed by a Covenantor (Parent) resident in England, Wales or Northern Ireland.

DEED OF COVENANT
I [*name of person making covenant*]
of [*address of person making covenant*]
covenant to pay my son/daughter [*full name of child*]
of [*address of child*]
the sum of £...... (gross) on
[*state date or dates*] in each year, for the period of seven years, or for the period of our joint lives, or until he/she ceases to be receiving full-time education at any university, college, school or other educational establishment (whichever is the shortest period) the first payment to be made on
.... Date ....

Signed, sealed and delivered by
[*signature of person making covenant*]
in the presence of [*witness's signature and address*]
Person making the covenant

Please state below the Tax District (and reference number) which deals with your tax affairs
District .... Reference ....

Providing the adult student's other income is less than his or her personal allowance, all or part of the Income Tax deducted by the parent is repayable. The income received under a deed of covenant is not counted in assessing the amount of any educational grant to which the student may be entitled.

Payments under court order

We have already seen in Chapter 7 that on the breakdown of a marriage a considerable saving in tax can often be achieved by structuring the amount of maintenance payable by the husband in such a way that a proportion is paid to his children. They then claim their personal allowances against the court order payments.

9

THE OVERSEAS ELEMENT

So far we have only been concerned with the tax position of individuals permanently resident in the United Kingdom. In this chapter I shall concentrate on some of the opportunities for tax planning which present themselves to those persons taking up employment overseas and to those individuals coming to work in the U.K.

Domicile and residence

The two concepts of domicile and residence are of fundamental importance in determining the extent of an individual's liability to U.K. taxation. Their significance is not just confined to Income Tax but also to Capital Gains Tax and Capital Transfer Tax.

Whereas your residence status is dependent upon physical presence in the U.K., your domicile will generally be the country or state which you regard as your permanent homeland. For the majority of people this is their country of birth. You can abandon your original domicile by birth if you settle in another country or state with a view to making it your new permanent home. Providing you sever all links with the country where you were born you will acquire a domicile of choice in the new country. A wife's domicile is not dependent on that of her husband if they were married at some time after the end of 1973. Prior to that time a wife's domicile was the same as her husband's.

If you think you have good grounds for believing that you should not be regarded as domiciled in the U.K. you should write to your tax office about this. Usually, you can then expect to receive a questionnaire which you should fill in and send back to your tax office. The information you have supplied will be considered by the Inland Revenue's Specialist Department which deals with these matters before you are given a ruling on your status. Later on in this chapter we shall see how much more favourably individuals not domiciled in the U.K. are taxed on their overseas earnings and investment income.

All of you that permanently live and work in the U.K. are regarded as both resident and ordinarily resident for the purposes of U.K. taxation. Whenever you go abroad for just short periods your residence status is unaffected.

A visitor to this country will generally not become resident here unless the stay in a tax year lasts longer than six months. If on the other hand the visitor establishes a pattern of regular visits, U.K. residence will usually be established when the average time spent here comes to at least ninety days a year over a four year period.

Should the overseas visitor have a home in the U.K. which is available for his or her use the visitor will be resident here every year in which he or she sets foot in the U.K. This does not apply if the visitor is engaged in some full-time occupation overseas.

Going non-resident

The dual incentives of high salaries and low taxation may prompt you to decide to apply for a job overseas. This may involve living permanently abroad for a time. Your likely residence status is clearly set out in paragraph 18 of the Inland Revenue booklet IR20 – 'Residents and Non-Residents Liability to Tax in the United Kingdom' – as follows:

> 'If a person goes abroad for full-time service under a contract of employment and:
>
> (a) All the duties of his employment are performed

abroad or any duties he performs here are incidental to his duties abroad; and

(b) His absence from the U.K. in this employment is for a period which includes a complete tax year; and

(c) Interim visits to the U.K. do not amount to 6 months or more in any tax year or 3 months or more on average,

he is normally regarded as not resident and not ordinarily resident in the U.K. from the day following the date of his departure until the day preceding the date of his return.'

Just before you depart to take up your overseas assignment, write to your tax office and tell them of your plans. You will be sent a Form P85 to complete. This will tell your tax office whether your overseas employment is full-time, where you will be staying abroad, and how long you expect to remain away. It also asks whether your wife is accompanying you and what, if any, income you will be receiving in the U.K. while you are abroad. For example, you might arrange to let your house until you come back. The income from the letting will be taxable in the U.K. The amount of income on which you will pay tax is calculated in the same way as that set out in Chapter 6.

If you take up an overseas employment part way through a tax year you will normally be due an Income Tax repayment. This is because you are entitled to a full year's personal allowances for the period up to the date of departure. By that time you will only have received a proportion of these in calculating the monthly deduction of PAYE from your salary.

Tax saver

The astute would-be expatriate will realize that some of the potential opportunities for tax planning afforded by an overseas appointment need to be acted upon before departure. This is particularly so where the would-be expatriate is a married man and his wife is staying at home to look after their young children. While he becomes non-resident from the date of his departure she remains resident in the U.K. and reverts back to being taxed as a single person. Where she is looking after children she can also claim the additional personal allowance. If she does not work while her husband is abroad she will lose the benefit of her personal allowances unless she has some income against which to offset them. It is in these circumstances that the husband should transfer to his wife before he goes abroad those income-producing assets where she can reclaim the tax deducted from the income by set-off against her personal allowances. Generally, it is where the husband has a portfolio of shares that transfer of the ownership of these to his wife produces a more favourable tax treatment. This is because his dividend income will remain taxable in the U.K. while he is abroad. At best he would only be able to reclaim part of the tax back under a Double Tax Agreement between the United Kingdom and his new country of residence.

As a general guide you will not have to pay U.K. tax on any overseas income you receive while you are abroad. You might choose to invest part of your savings in one of the many U.K. Government Securities where the interest is free of U.K. tax when owned by a non-resident.

Before you return to take up U.K. residence again there are some specific tax-planning points which must be considered. For example, any deposit accounts should be closed before you return as you could otherwise face the prospect of a charge to U.K. Income Tax on interest received during your period of non-residence.

Taking up U.K. residence

If you have just arrived in this country you are probably anxious to know how much tax you will have to pay each year. In view of my comments at the beginning of the chapter you should initially be able to satisfy our Inland Revenue Authorities that you have an overseas domicile. Any income from investments here is taxable as it arises, but your overseas investment income is not taxed unless it is actually remitted here.

Where your job is with either a U.K. or overseas employer and the duties of your employment are performed wholly in the U.K., the full amount of your salary is taxable here. If you were working for a foreign employer in the U.K. before 14 March 1984 and have not been resident here for nine out of the ten years prior to 1984/85 you are only taxed on 50% of your earnings in the U.K. You can of course claim any U.K. personal allowances to which you are entitled.

Illustration

A married couple, domiciled overseas, came to live in the U.K. in 1982. The husband is employed by a foreign employer. His earnings during 1984/85 were £30,000. The U.K. Income Tax payable for the year amounts to £3,553.50, as follows:

	£
Earned income	30,000
Less: Deduction – 50%	15,000
	15,000
Personal allowance	3,155
Taxable income	£11,845
1984/85 Tax payable at 30%	£3,553.50

While you live here you might still have to complete a Tax Return in your overseas country of origin and pay taxes there as well. If it is one of the countries which have concluded a Double Tax Agreement with the U.K. you should not have to pay tax twice on the same income.

10

CAPITAL GAINS TAX

True to its name, Capital Gains Tax is a tax on capital profits. As with most other forms of taxation there is the usual list of exceptions to this general rule. Gambling or pools winnings and personal or professional damages are not taxable. Neither are gains realized on disposing of any of the assets in the following table:

Private cars
National Savings
Your private residence
Chattels, with an expected life of more than fifty years, sold for less than £3,000
British government securities held for at least twelve months
Life assurance policies
Charitable gifts
Gifts for the public benefit
Standing timber
Foreign currency for personal expenditure.

In addition, for the year 1984/85 the first £5,600 of chargeable gains are exempt from tax. The excess is charged at the flat rate of 30%. Like the main personal allowances the annual exemption limit goes up each year in line with the movement in the Retail Prices Index during the previous calendar year.

The indexation allowance
This allowance measures the impact of inflation on both the cost of an asset and any other expenditure incurred on

enhancing its value. No allowance is due:

(1) Where an asset is sold within twelve months of acquisition, or
(2) For any part of the period of ownership up until March 1982, or
(3) An asset is sold at a loss.

Neither can the indexation allowance turn a gain into a loss. It can only reduce it to nil.

The allowance is governed by the movement in the Retail Prices Index in the period between the first anniversary after an asset is acquired and its date of sale. For assets which you have owned since before April 1981 the starting date for calculating the indexation allowance is March 1982. Table 6 at the end of the book sets out the indexation allowance for assets disposed of between April and December 1984.

Illustration

A property purchased in 1978 for £25,000 was sold in May 1984 for £36,000. The indexation allowance between March 1982 and May 1984 is 0.120.

The chargeable gain is calculated as follows:

	£	£
Proceeds of sale		36,000
Less: Purchase price	25,000	
Indexation allowance: £25,000×0.120	3,000	
		28,000
Chargeable gain		£8,000

If the property had been bought in August 1982 the indexation allowance would be due from August 1983 up to the sale in May 1984.

Husband and wife

In the year of marriage husband and wife each remain taxable as single persons. Both of them can realize chargeable gains up to the limit of the exempt amount without incurring a charge to Capital Gains Tax. Thereafter the exemption limit of £5,600 is divisible between them on a pro rata basis depending on the gains they make in a tax year. Losses made by one spouse can be set against gains realized by the other in the same or subsequent years. Unless the couple elect for separate assessment for Capital Gains Tax the husband is responsible for paying the tax on both his own and his wife's gains. So long as the married couple are living together, assets can be transferred between them without incurring a charge to tax. The amount of any indexation allowance up to the time of transfer must be worked out. The calculation of the allowance due to the transferee on an eventual disposal of an asset is more complicated. When a couple permanently separate from one another the ability to transfer assets between them free of tax is lost.

The computation of gains

The taxable gain on the disposal of an asset is calculated by making various deductions from the price realized on sale, as follows:

(1) The cost of acquisition, and

(2) The incidental costs of buying and selling the asset, and

(3) Any additional expenditure incurred on enhancing the value of the asset during the period of ownership, and

(4) The indexation allowance.

There are occasions when a different figure from the actual disposal proceeds is substituted in the calculation. For example, this happens when you make a gift or sell an asset at a nominal value to a close member of your family. You must then bring into the computation of the capital gain the open-market value of the asset at the time of disposal.

The date of sale of an asset is taken as the date when the contract for sale is made.

Illustration

A property was purchased in 1979 for £30,000. The costs of purchase, including solicitor's fees and Stamp Duty, came to £1,100. In 1980 central heating was installed for £1,500. Contracts for sale were exchanged in June 1984 and the sale was completed in July 1984. The property was sold for £55,000. The agent's commission amounted to £1,265 and the solicitor's fees came to £345. The indexation allowance between March 1982 and June 1984 is 0.123.

The chargeable gain is calculated as follows:

	£	£
Proceeds of sale		55,000
Less: Agent's and solicitor's fees		1,610
		53,390
Less: Purchase price	30,000	
Costs of purchase	1,100	
Expenditure on improvements	1,500	
	32,600	
Indexation allowance: £32,600×0.123	4,010	
		36,610
Chargeable gain		£16,780

Losses

We have already seen that where an asset is sold at a loss no indexation allowance is given. Losses can be set against gains made in the same year. Where the result for the year is an overall loss it can be carried forward to be set against gains in a later year without time limit. It then reduces the amount of your gains which exceed the exemption limit, as follows:

Illustration

A taxpayer had capital losses of £1,860 available for carry-forward at 5 April 1984. During 1984/85 the taxpayer realized gains of £7,270 and made losses of £610.

The capital gains position for the year is:

	£	£
Gains realized in the year		7,270
Less: Losses: in the year	610	
brought forward (part)	1,060	
		1,670
1984/85 Exemption limit		£5,600

The unused losses of £800 can be carried forward to be set against gains in later years.

A loss arising on the sale or gift of an asset to a person connected with the transferor can only be set against a gain from a similar disposal at some time in the future. Where the value of an asset you own becomes negligible or nil you can claim the loss without actually disposing of the asset. If you have subscribed for shares in a trading company which are not quoted on a recognized stock exchange and you make a loss on selling them or they become worthless, you can set this loss against your income rather than against your other capital gains.

Tax saver

Your private residence

The profit on a sale of your home is exempt from tax. The exemption extends to the house and its garden or grounds up to one acre, including the land on which the house is built. A larger area can qualify for exemption where it can be shown that it was needed to enjoy the house. Where a home has not been occupied as your private residence throughout the full period of ownership, a proportion of the gain on sale becomes taxable. Nevertheless, certain periods of absence are disregarded in determining whether the gain is totally exempt from tax. These are the last twenty-four months of ownership in any event and generally those when you have to live away from home because of your work.

Where part of your home is used exclusively for business purposes the proportion of the profit on sale attributable to the business use is a chargeable gain. Whether part of your home is actually used exclusively for business use is entirely a matter of fact.

If you let part of your home as residential accommodation the gain on the part which has been let is either wholly or partly exempt from tax. The proportion of the profit on sale which is exempt is the lower of either £20,000 or an amount equivalent to the gain on the part you have occupied as your home. Alternatively, if you take in lodgers who mix in and eat with your family, the Inland Revenue take the view that no part of the exemption on a sale of your home is lost.

A second home

If you have two homes such as a house or flat in town for use during the weekdays and a cottage in the country for weekends, the profit on sale of only one of them is exempt from tax. Which one counts as your main residence is a matter of fact. It is, however, possible for you to determine this by writing to your tax office. In the election you should request which of your homes you want to be regarded as your principal private residence for Capital Gains Tax purposes. The election can start to apply from any time in the two years up to the date it is made. You are, of course, free to vary it as and when it suits you.

If you own a home which is occupied rent-free by a dependent relative then the profit on sale is tax-free.

Stocks and shares

Prior to 6 April 1982 each shareholding was regarded as a single asset. This was commonly known as a 'pool'. Each additional purchase of the same class of shares or a sale of part of the holding either represented an addition to, or a disposal out of, the pool. With the introduction of the indexation allowance this has now changed. Each shareholding acquired after 5 April 1982 now represents a separate asset. A subsequent addition to a holding you owned at 5 April 1982 cannot be added to the pool.

There is a set procedure for matching shares sold with their corresponding acquisition, as follows:

(1) Shares acquired in the same stock exchange account subject to certain exceptions
(2) Shares acquired within the twelve months preceding a disposal on a first-in first-out basis
(3) Shares acquired more than twelve months before a disposal on a last-in first-out basis.

Illustration

A taxpayer had the following transactions in the shares of a public company:

	£
August 1976: 500 bought for	1,300
January 1980: 700 bought for	1,200
Pool: 1,200 costing	2,500
October 1983: 1,000 bought for	2,000
May 1984: 500 sold for	1,200
June 1984: 900 sold for	2,700

The indexation allowance between March 1982 and June 1984 is 0.123.
(1) The sale in May 1984 is identified with part of the holding bought in October 1983:

Sale proceeds of 500 shares	1,200
Cost of shares sold: 500/1,000×£2,000	1,000
Chargeable gain	£200

(2) The shares sold in June 1984 are matched with the balance of the holding purchased in October 1983 and part of the pooled holding on 5 April 1982:

(a) Sale proceeds: 500/900×£2,700	1,500
Cost of shares sold: 500/1,000×£2,000	1,000
Chargeable gain	£500
(b) Sale proceeds: 400/900×£2,700	1,200
Cost of shares sold: 400/1,200×£2,500	833
	367
Less: Indexation allowance 0.123×£833	102
Chargeable gain	£265

Where a company in which you have a holding is taken over, and instead of receiving cash you exchange your shares for a holding in the new company, no disposal takes place at that time. Your new holding is regarded as having been acquired at the same time and for the same price as the old one.

Chattels

Gains on the sales of chattels with an expected life of more than fifty years sold for less than £3,000 are exempt from tax. For items which fetch between £3,000 and £7,500 the chargeable gain is restricted to 5/3 times the amount of the proceeds of sale (ignoring expenses) over £3,000 where this is to the taxpayer's advantage.

Illustration

A piece of antique furniture purchased in 1972 for £830 was sold in August 1983 for £5,400. Although the profit on sale was £4,570 the chargeable gain is restricted to £4,000, being 5/3×(£5,400–£3,000).

Where an article is sold at a loss for under £3,000, the allowable loss is restricted by assuming the proceeds on sale were equivalent to £3,000.

Illustration

A painting was purchased many years ago for £6,320. It subsequently transpired that it was a fake and was sold for £90. The loss on sale is restricted to £3,320, being £6,320 less £3,000.

Articles comprising a set are regarded as a single item when they are sold to the same person but at different times.

Wasting assets

Wasting assets are assets with an expected life span of less than fifty years. Unless it comes within the definition of 'tangible moveable property' a gain on the sale of a wasting asset is calculated in the same way as that on the sale of any other asset, except that the purchase price wastes away during the asset's expected life span. Leases of land for less than fifty years are wasting assets. A specific table is provided for calculating the proportion of the purchase price of a lease which can be deducted from the sale proceeds.

The gain on a sale of a wasting asset which is also 'tangible moveable property' is exempt from tax. Neither does a loss on a sale of similar property count as an allowable loss.

Part disposals

Where you only sell part of an asset its acquisition cost is apportioned between the part sold and the proportion retained. This is done on a pro rata basis by reference to the proceeds of sale of the part sold and the open-market value of the proportion retained. The indexation allowance is calculated on the cost of the part sold. The proportion of the original cost of the asset attributable to the part which was not sold can be set against the proceeds on a sale of the remainder at a later date.

Business assets

If you are in business and dispose of an asset used in your trade you have to pay Capital Gains Tax on the profit on sale. The profit or loss is calculated in the same way as that on a disposal of an asset you own personally. If the proceeds of sale are reinvested wholly or partly in other assets for use in the business, payment of the tax on the profit can be wholly or partly postponed. This is achieved by reducing the cost of the replacement assets by the capital gain realized on the disposal of the old asset.

When you come to dispose of your business assets on retirement either by sale or gift the first £100,000 of capital gains is exempt from tax. To qualify for this maximum exemption you must have been in business for at least ten years and be over age 65 at the time of the disposal. The age qualification applies equally to both sexes. If you retire between ages 60 and 65 the exemption is reduced to £20,000 for every year by which you are more than 60 years old at the time. For every month you delay retiring, a fraction of £20,000 is added to the calculation of your exemption limit. Your maximum relief for Capital Gains Tax on retirement is also restricted where you have not been in business for ten years.

The precise rules which apply in calculating the capital gain on the disposal of a business asset during the course of trading or on retirement are complicated. It is outside the scope of this book for me to go into them in detail. The indexation allowance features in both of them.

Gifts

Where there is a capital gain on an asset you give away you can elect with the transferee for payment of the tax to be postponed until the asset is subsequently disposed of by the transferee. The amount of the gain on the transfer is reduced by the indexation allowance which is due at the time. The transferee must keep the asset for at least a year before any further indexation allowance is given on the subsequent disposal.

Inheritances

No Capital Gains Tax is payable on the unrealized profits on your assets at the date of your death. When you inherit an asset you acquire it at the value on the date of death of the deceased. Generally, this rule is also applied whenever you become entitled to assets from a trust. As the trustees will usually be liable to Capital Gains Tax on the unrealized gains at the time of transfer, payment of the tax can be postponed in a similar way to that which applies on gifts. You have to join in with the trusteees in making this election.

Assets held on 6 April 1965

Apart from quoted stocks and shares, a gain on the sale of an asset which you have owned since before 6 April 1965 is reduced. This is done to eliminate from the charge to tax the profit on sale attributable to the period up to 5 April 1965, the date when Capital Gains Tax was introduced. This reduction is achieved by assuming the gain was made evenly on a time basis throughout the period of ownership. The taxable part of the gain is determined as follows:

$$\frac{\text{Period of time from 6 April 1965 to the date of sale}}{\text{Period of time from acquisition to the date of sale}} \times \text{Overall gain}$$

Alternatively, it is possible for you to elect for the value of the asset on 6 April 1965 to be substituted in the calculation of the capital gain arising on sale. You will choose to make this election in writing to your tax office where your taxable gain comes out at a lower figure.

Illustration

A property purchased in May 1962 for £3,000 was sold in May 1984 for £30,000. On 6 April 1965 it had a value of £9,000. The indexation allowance between March 1982 and May 1984 is 0.120.

The first calculation of the chargeable gain is:

	£	£
Sale proceeds		30,000
Less: Purchase price	3,000	
Indexation allowance £3,000×0.120	360	
		3,360
Gross gain		£26,640

Time apportionment:

$$\frac{\text{April 1965 to May 1984} = 229 \text{ months}}{\text{May 1962 to May 1984} = 264 \text{ months}} \times £26{,}640 = £23{,}108$$

The second calculation of the chargeable gain is:

	£	£
Sale proceeds		30,000
Less: 6 April 1965 value	9,000	
Indexation allowance £9,000×0.120	1,080	
		10,080
Chargeable gain		£19,920

It is to the taxpayer's advantage to make an election for the 6 April 1965 value to be used in calculating the capital gain.

Perhaps you still own some quoted investments which were purchased before 6 April 1965. You may already have elected for them to be regarded as if they had been bought on 6 April 1965 at their market value at that date. If this is so then any additions to, or part disposals of, these shareholdings up until 5 April 1982 were treated as a pool in the way described in an earlier section in this chapter. If no election has been made to use the 6 April 1965 value then the profit or loss on sale is found by comparing the sale proceeds with either the original cost of the investment or its value on 6 April 1965. The chargeable gain is the lower of the two figures. If one calculation results in a gain and the other throws up a loss, the transaction is treated as giving rise to neither gain nor loss.

11

COMPLETING THE RETURN

When you collect your post up from the doormat you can always pick out your Tax Return from the other letters. It comes in a distinctive brown envelope at the same time every year. Try to avoid the temptation to put it to one side. Although it might not prove possible to complete the Return and send it back to your tax office within the required thirty days, it is better to deal with it promptly. At least your tax office can then see that you are being given the correct allowances and reliefs in the code number which your employer is using to calculate the regular deductions for PAYE from your salary or wages. If your Return shows that you owe some additional tax on your income or you have realized some capital gains, the Inspector of Taxes will send you any assessments to collect the tax due. Failure to deal with your Tax Return quickly can often result in the Inland Revenue sending you assessments showing your income has been estimated. What you do when you receive one of these is dealt with in Chapter 12.

Not everyone is sent a Tax Return. If you do not receive one it is probably because your tax office think your only income is your salary or wage taxed under PAYE. If this is so and you are satisfied you are being given all the personal allowances and reliefs which you can claim you need do nothing more. On the other hand, if you have received additional income which is taxable you should ask for a Tax Return so you can declare it to the Inland Revenue and pay any tax due on it. Failure to do this will lead to the imposition of both interest and penalties.

There are several different types of Income Tax Return. The

following list shows which one you can expect to receive:

Form Number	*Classification of Taxpayer*
11	Standard full return for self-employed person
11P	Standard full return for employee
11K	Non-domiciled individual
P1	Simplified return for employee
R40	Taxpayer entitled to a repayment
R232	Minors repayment claim

With your Tax Return comes a 'Tax Return Guide' which will help you complete the form. A Tax Return form is reproduced in Chapter 14, filled out by a fictional character.

This book is being published at about the time you should be receiving your 1985/86 Tax Return. You may well ask why the Return refers to the tax year which has just started rather than the one which has just finished. The answer is that the form serves two purposes. It acts as a report of your income, outgoings and capital gains for the year ended on 5 April 1985, but the section on allowances is for the year to 5 April 1986.

As there is not a great deal of space in each section of the Return you can always provide more detailed information on a separate statement and only show the total income for a particular item on the form. When you do this every item on your Return for which there is a supporting statement should be noted 'see schedule attached' or words to that effect.

Let us now go through the sections in the form to understand what needs to be shown under the various headings and where you will be able to find this information. Remember if you are a married man you must also give full details of your wife's income, outgoings and capital gains. When the Return is finished it must be signed in the space provided on the front page. Bear in mind the wording of the Declaration: 'To the best of my knowledge and belief the particulars given on this form are correct and complete.

Income

Form P60 – your certificate of pay and tax deducted – given to you by your employer shortly after the end of the tax year will tell you the amount of your salary or wages to enter on the Tax Return. You should keep this form so that if you receive a formal assessment on your earnings you can check the figure of tax deducted from them with that shown on the P60. If you are a company director or earn more than £8,500 per annum your employer will complete a Form P11D detailing your benefits-in-kind and other expenses payments. You should ask for a copy of this and enter your taxable benefits. Where you spent more than thirty days abroad on business you should compile a list of the dates spent away, the places visited, the purpose of each trip and the number of qualifying days for this purpose. This list should be sent in with your Tax Return. Use this part of the form to claim relief for any expenses, such as professional subscriptions, incurred in connection with your employment.

If you are self-employed you will have to prepare a statement of the income and expenses from your business. You should do this along the lines set out in Chapter 5. On the Return Form you should enter the nature of your business and its address.

The amount of your pension from a previous employer's pension fund will also be notified to you on a Form P60. If either you or your wife are drawing the National Insurance Retirement Pension or some other benefit from the State you should declare the amount of your income for the 52-week period to 5 April 1985. Particularly where your National Insurance Pension is paid quarterly there will be a small difference between the income you should show on the Return and the actual pension received during the tax year. Some State benefits are exempt from tax. These are shown in Table 7 at the end of the book.

Your managing agents will have regularly sent you statements showing the rents receivable and expenses incurred for any properties which you let out. From these you should prepare a summary to accompany your Tax Return along the lines set out in Chapter 6.

The amount of interest earned during the year on your bank deposit account can be obtained from your bank statements. Most banks credit interest half-yearly at the end of each June and December. If you receive your interest at more regular intervals or had a large sum on deposit for short fixed periods you must make sure that the interest from all your accounts is reported on the Tax Return.

There is also a section in which to enter the amount of any building society interest received. You can normally obtain this information from your pass book. If you have an account which pays interest monthly you will need to enter the total of all your monthly receipts.

Dividends on your shareholdings come with counterfoils. These should always be kept. You can then list them and just enter on the Tax Return the total of all your dividends and tax credits during the tax year. The list should be sent in with the Tax Return. The same procedure should be followed where you are receiving fixed-interest payments from which tax is deducted at source.

If you are fortunate enough to be receiving income from a trust, the trustee will send you a certificate showing your income each year. You should enter the gross amount in the space provided in the Return.

There are other sections in the part of your Return dealing with your income but they are unlikely to be of general application.

Outgoings

This part of the Return is almost entirely devoted to your borrowings and the interest paid on these. The purposes for which you can take out a loan and get tax relief on the interest are set out in Chapter 3. Make sure you attach to the Tax Return any certificate of interest paid where this is relevant.

Details of all the covenants you have taken out need to be entered on the Return. You should include the gross amounts for all your covenanted payments including any charitable ones.

If you are making payments to a former or separated wife there is a space for these to be entered. This also applies to amounts you are paying to your children under a court order. Again, it is the gross amounts which need to be reported.

Capital gains

Every time you buy or sell shares or securities your broker sends you a contract note. Do not lose these as you will need them to complete this part of the Return. In order that any Capital Gains Tax due from you can be calculated, enter on the Return details of all the assets you sold during the tax year. Even if you think a profit on sale is exempt from tax, still report the sale in this section. Where your total chargeable gains, before losses, are less than £5,600 and the total proceeds of all your sales during the year are under £11,200 it will normally be sufficient to write in this section of the Return: 'gains not exceeding £5,600 and disposal proceeds not exceeding £11,200'.

Details of all chargeable assets acquired during the year should be included in the space given over to these.

Allowances

All the various personal allowances are set out in this part of the Return Form. In each case there is a space for you to enter the information the Inland Revenue need to tell whether you are entitled to be given the allowance. You will be well advised to look through each section carefully. I suggest you refer back to Chapter 2 which dealt with the various personal allowances and who can claim them.

Penalties

Earlier in this chapter I made a passing reference to the powers of the Inland Revenue to impose interest and penalties. This will happen if you omit to tell your tax office about some source of income or capital gain or fail to submit your Tax Returns promptly. Making an incomplete or incorrect Tax Return or statement is also a serious offence which will lead to the levy of a penalty. The maximum penalties which are prescribed are:

Offence	*Penalty*
Failure to notify liability to tax within one year after the end of the tax year in which it arises	£100
Failure to complete a Tax Return	£50, plus a possible extra £10 a day. Where the failure continues beyond the end of the tax year after that in which the Return was issued the penalty is increased to £50 plus the tax payable based on the Return.
Making an incorrect Return or statement	£50, plus the amount of tax lost by the Inland Revenue. In the case of fraud the penalty is increased to twice the amount of tax lost.

The Inland Revenue will usually charge a penalty below the maximum limit. This depends on the seriousness of the offence and other circumstances. In addition to charging a penalty the Inland Revenue will also claim interest. This will be calculated from the date when the tax was normally due. These dates are set out in Chapter 12.

12

ASSESSMENTS AND REPAYMENT CLAIMS

If you ignore an assessment of demand sent to you by the Inland Revenue, the end result can come as an unpleasant surprise. Your responsibilities as a taxpayer are not just confined to completing your Tax Return each year. It is also important you understand what action you need to take whenever you receive an assessment and how to claim any repayment due to you.

Appeals

Each assessment sent to you will tell you how long you have in which to appeal against it. This time limit is usually thirty days. If you are late in dealing with the Return you run the risk of assessments being sent to you by the Inland Revenue which require some action within this appeal period. Providing you complete your Tax Return promptly it is less likely that any assessments you receive will be inaccurate.

The Inland Revenue have a special Form 64–7 for giving an appeal against an assessment. One of these forms will usually be sent to you with each assessment. You are not bound to use it: if you prefer to make your objection in a letter this will do. What is important is that your appeal should clearly state the reasons why you disagree with the assessment. This will usually be because the Inland Revenue have estimated your income or business profits in the absence of your Tax Return or accounts. Where the assessment is excessive you should say so in your appeal. Alternatively, if it is not in accordance with information already sent, or to be provided, to the Inland Revenue then this will be the basis of your appeal. Wherever possible try and send the Inland Revenue the missing Return or outstanding information as soon as you can.

Inevitably the incorrect assessment shows you owe some tax. Where you think this is more than the amount which will ultimately be payable you should request that collection of the excess be postponed. Do this at the same time as your appeal. You must specify your reasons why you want all or part of the tax charged on the assessment postponed. Unless an application for postponement is made all the tax will be due and payable on the date shown on the assessment.

The majority of appeals are eventually settled by agreement between the taxpayer and the Inland Revenue. The assessment will then be adjusted to the agreed figures. There are occasions when agreement cannot be reached. The procedure for resolving your appeal starts with a hearing before the General Tax Commissioners. It can then move on to the Courts and ultimately to the House of Lords.

Should you ever reach the stage of receiving notification of a hearing of an appeal before the General Commissioners you ignore it at your peril. This is because the Commissioners have the power to determine your appeal. Unless you are represented at the hearing you can end up paying more than the true amount of tax due on the assessment.

Normal dates for tax payments

For the tax year 1984/85 these are:

Type of Assessment	*Date of payment*
Income Tax and Class 4 National Insurance contributions on business profits	Half on 1 January 1985, half on 1 July 1985
Income Tax on rents and untaxed interest	1 January 1985
Higher rate tax and investment income surcharge on taxed investment income	1 December 1985
Capital gains tax	1 December 1985

Interest on overdue tax

If you delay paying your tax after it is due you face the prospect of being charged interest. The current rate is 8% per annum. The interest is calculated from the due date up until payment. Except where an appeal is given against an assessment the due date will either be one of those in the preceding section in this chapter or thirty days after the assessment is issued if that is later. Where the interest is less than £30 it will not normally be collected.

Repayment claims

There are a number of situations which can lead to a tax refund. This can simply arise because you have paid more tax than you should have done. Alternatively, perhaps your business had a bad year and made a loss. A repayment would be due to you by setting the loss against other income on which tax had already been paid. In these situations the Inland Revenue will send your refund as soon as they receive a request for repayment from you.

There are also those taxpayers whose income mainly comes from investments. When they come to claim their personal allowances they will usually end up receiving an income tax repayment.

Illustration

A single woman had an income from dividends of £2,800 net during 1984/85. She also received building society interest of £700 and her earnings from a part-time employment were £800.

	Income	*Tax deducted*
	£	£
Casual earnings	800	
Dividends	4,000	1,200.00
Building society interest	1,000	300.00
	5,800	1,500.00
Less: Personal allowance	2,005	
Taxable income	£3,795	

Tax thereon:	
£3,795 at 30%	1,138.50
1984/85 repayment	£361.50

Repayment supplement

Whenever the Inland Revenue refund more than £25 they have to work out whether to supplement it by a payment of interest. The current rate is 8% per annum and the supplement is not taxable. It is calculated from one of two dates, whichever is the later. The first is the end of the tax year following the one for which the repayment is due. The second is the end of the year of assessment in which the tax was paid.

Remission of tax

Tax saver

There are occasions when the Inland Revenue do not act promptly after they receive your Tax Return or other information about a change in your circumstances. Where there is no response from the tax office it is not unreasonable for you to believe that your affairs are in order. If you were subsequently faced with a large demand which had built up through this sort of oversight it could cause you considerable hardship.

In recognition of this the Inland Revenue will not collect all the arrears of tax which have built up because of a failure to make proper and timely use of information supplied by the taxpayer. The amount you are let off depends on the size of your income when you are notified of the arrears. From 1 August 1984 the following table applies:

Gross Income			
Under 65	*Over 65*	*Remit*	*Collect*
up to £8,000	up to £10,500	All	None
£8,001–£10,000	£10,501–£12,500	75%	25%
£10,001–£12,500	£12,501–£15,000	50%	50%
£12,501–£15,000	£15,001–£17,500	25%	75%
£15,001–£21,500	£17,501–£24,000	10%	90%

13

CAPITAL TRANSFER TAX

In previous chapters we have seen the impact that taxation can have both on income and on capital profits. If you give some of your assets away during your lifetime, once again taxation plays a part in the transaction. Only a proportion of your gift will end up in the beneficiary's hands and the remainder will go to the Inland Revenue in payment of the Capital Transfer Tax due on the gift. Not only is it payable on transfers or gifts you make during your lifetime but also on the value of your estate on death. Unlike the rules which apply for Income Tax, husband and wife are treated as separate individuals. Both are entitled to the various exemptions. Many of the principles and workings to do with Capital Transfer Tax are far from straightforward. What follows is only a brief outline.

Your annual Tax Return only makes a reference to Capital Transfer Tax and points out when you need to make a Return to the Capital Taxes Office. This is done on one of two special forms: C–5 or C–6.

Rates of tax

Each gift or transfer is not considered in isolation in calculating how much tax is payable on it. In working out how much is payable, previous transfers are taken into account. This is because the tax due on each gift or the value of your estate on death is dependent upon the cumulative value of all other transfers chargeable to Capital Transfer Tax in the ten years leading up to the date of the next chargeable transfer.

There are two different rates of tax. Lifetime gifts are taxed at rates lower than those payable on an estate on death. Transfers in the three years prior to death are also charged to tax at the rates on death. The rates of Capital Transfer Tax payable on lifetime gifts and deaths from 13 March 1984 are:

Lifetime transfers

Cumulative gross Chargeable transfers	*Rate*	*Tax on Band*	*Cumulative Tax*
£	%	£	£
0– 64,000	0	Nil	Nil
64,001– 85,000	15	3,150	3,150
85,001– 116,000	17.5	5,425	8,575
116,001– 148,000	20	6,400	14,975
148,001– 185,000	22.5	8,325	23,300
185,001– 232,000	25	11,750	35,050
232,001– 285,000	27.5	14,575	49,625
over 285,000	30		

Transfers on death

Cumulative gross Chargeable transfers	*Rate*	*Tax on Band*	*Cumulative Tax*
£	%	£	£
0– 64,000	0	Nil	Nil
64,001– 85,000	30	6,300	6,300
85,001– 116,000	35	10,850	17,150
116,001– 148,000	40	12,800	29,950
148,001– 185,000	45	16,650	46,600
185,001– 232,000	50	23,500	70,100
232,001– 285,000	55	29,150	99,250
over 285,000	60		

Like the main personal Income Tax allowances, both the limit of £64,000 on chargeable transfers taxable at a nil rate and the other rate bands go up each year. The increase is measured by the movement in the Retail Prices Index during the previous calendar year. A rounding-up adjustment may be necessary.

Illustration

In December 1984 a married man decided to make a taxable gift of £10,000. In previous years his chargeable transfers were £90,000. He retained £1,750 (£10,000×17.5%) to pay the Capital Transfer Tax on the gift and gave the remainder of £8,250 away.

Exemptions

There are a number of transfers which are exempt from Capital Transfer Tax. The main ones which apply to individuals are:

(1) Gifts up to £3,000 in any one tax year. Any part of the exemption which is left over can be carried forward to the following year only. For example, if your total transfers came to £1,500 during 1983/84 you could have given away as much as £4,500 during 1984/85, all within your annual exemption limit.

(2) Gifts to any one person up to £250 per person in each tax year. Where the total amount given to any one individual exceeds this limit no part comes within this exemption.

(3) Marriage gifts. To fall within this exemption the gift must be in consideration of marriage. The amount you can give away depends on your relationship to the bride or bridegroom as follows:

	£
By either parent	5,000
By a grandparent or great-grandparent	2,500
By bridegroom to bride or vice versa	2,500
By any other person	1,000

(4) Regular gifts out of income which form part of your normal expenditure.

(5) Gifts and bequests to charities without limit.

(6) Gifts to political parties, although this exemption is limited to £100,000 where these are on, or within one year of, death.

(7) Transfers between husband and wife.

Miscellaneous aspects

If you own shares in a family company or have your own business then the value of these assets is reduced in calculating how much Capital Transfer Tax is due on them when you give them away, or if they are included in your estate when you die. Interests in agricultural property or woodlands are also more generously treated than most other assets.

It is also worth noting that Capital Transfer Tax can apply in varying ways to different types of trust.

14

THE TAX AFFAIRS OF JOHN SMITH – A CASE STUDY

The story

This is the story of John Smith and his family. John is employed as a salesman. His salary during 1984/85 was £20,200. He has a company car for which his employer pays all the running expenses. John's job often takes him overseas. He spent 37 qualifying days abroad on business during the last tax year.

John's wife Jean is self-employed. Her profits, as adjusted for tax purposes, for the years ended 30 June 1983 and 1984 were £10,000 and £8,000 respectively. She pays an annual premium of £1,000 into a personal pension policy.

Two years ago John and Jean bought a new house. They have a joint £25,000 endowment mortgage with a building society. John paid interest of £2,650 on this during 1984/85. The annual premium on the endowment policy is £800 gross.

Over the years they have both managed to save some of their income. John prefers to invest most of his savings in a bank deposit account. The interest on his account during 1983/84 and 1984/85 was £250 and £200 respectively. In May 1984 John purchased some shares in Moorfield Electrical Limited and Highfell Plastics Limited for £1,000 and £1,600 respectively. His net dividends were £140 for the last tax year. Jean's loyalties lie with the local building society. She earned interest of £70 in 1984/85.

The only deed of covenant John has taken out is in favour of the local church. He pays £100 gross each year under the deed.

John and Jean have two children. Last November their

daughter Sarah married her childhood sweetheart Stephen. Tom, their 19-year-old son, started a university degree course in October 1984. John also helps support his elderly mother-in-law Dorothy whose only income is her basic National Insurance Pension.

When David's father died ten years ago he left John his country cottage. At the time it was valued at £10,000. Since then John and Jean have installed central heating which cost them £1,000. Last year, now that their children are grown up, they decided to sell it. It was sold in September 1984 for £24,000. The solicitors' and estate agents' fees amounted to £920. John has not yet decided how to reinvest the proceeds of sale. In the meantime he has put them in a short-term deposit account for a fixed period of six months. It matured in March, and the interest amounted to £1,030.

John's 1985/86 Tax Return

This is reproduced on the following six pages.

John's tax liabilities for 1984/85

(1) Under PAYE

	£	£
Salary		20,200
Car benefit		750
Car fuel benefit		750
		21,700
Less: Allowances and reliefs		
Foreign earnings deduction:		
37/365 × £21,700 × 12.5%	275	
Personal allowance	3,155	
Dependent relative allowance	100	3,530
Taxable income		£18,170
Tax thereon:		
First £18,150 at 30%		5,445
Next £20 at 40%		8
Tax deductible under PAYE for 1984/85		£5,453

(text continues on p. 106)

SPECIMEN FORM

District

Tax Return 1985-1986

Date of issue

IN ANY ENQUIRY PLEASE QUOTE

▶ 191 / J273

John Smith, Esq.
34 Newfield Road,
Oldgate,
LR3 6PT

Income and Capital Gains for year ended 5 April 1985

Allowances for year ending 5 April 1986

You are required to complete pages 2–6 of this form, sign the Declaration below and send it back to me within 30 days. It will help if you will also give the information requested at the bottom of this page.

Please read the introduction to the enclosed notes before you start to fill in the form; the notes are there to help you. If you need further help or information please ask me.

H.M. Inspector of Taxes

Declaration

False statements can result in prosecution

To the best of my knowledge and belief the particulars given on this form are correct and complete.

Signature John Smith Date 19th May 1984.

A woman should state after her signature whether she is single, married, widowed, separated or divorced

Private address
Use CAPITAL letters 34 NEWFIELD ROAD
OLDGATE

Postcode LR3 6PT.

If you make the return as Executor, Trustee, Receiver, etc., state in what capacity and for whom made: ....

Pensions information – these details will help me to give you the right PAYE code

If you and/or your wife were born before 6 April 1926 please enter date(s) of birth ▼	*Please state here the current weekly/monthly/four weekly/quarterly rate of each Social Security or other pension you receive*	Nature of pension	Self	Wife	*State "Weekly" "Monthly" etc.*
			£	£	
			£	£	
			£	£	

Self	*If you or your wife are likely to begin receiving a pension before 6 April 1986 please state* ▶	Nature of pension ....
Wife		Starting on *(date)* ....
		Rate of pension .... per week/month/four weeks/quarter
		Payable to *(self or wife)* ....

SPECIMEN FORM

INCOME: Year 6 April 1984 to 5 April 1985

	See Note	Details	Amount for year Self	Amount for year Wife
Employments or offices	1	Occupation: SALESMAN — Employer's name and address: JONES LTD, SPENCER AVENUE, OLDGATE	£	£
	5–7	Earnings, (including fees, bonus, commission)	20,200	—
		Tips etc.		—
		Wife's earnings (including fees bonus, commission)	—	
		Tips etc.	—	
	8–9	Benefits, expense allowances — CAR BENEFIT	750	
	10	Leaving payments and compensation — CAR FUEL BENEFIT	750	
	11	*If you or your wife received a taxed sum from the trustees of an approved profit sharing scheme enter "X" here (See also Note 76)*	▶ ☐	▶ ☐
		If the sum is included with other income above also enter "X" here	▶ ☐	▶ ☐
	12	Duties performed abroad *Employment concerned* — SALESMAN FOR JONES LTD; Dates of absence *enclose statement if necessary* — AS SEPARATE STATEMENT - TOTAL 37 DAYS; Deduction claimed enter "X": 12½%	▶ X	▶ ☐
		Deduction claimed enter "X": 100%	▶ ☐	▶ ☐
		Expenses in employment	Amount for year Self £	Amount for year Wife £
	15	Details of expenses		
	16	Fees or subscriptions to professional bodies — Name of professional body		
Social Security pensions and benefits	20	Retirement pension or old person's pension — *If the pension, or any part of the pension your wife receives or is entitled to, arises by virtue of her own contributions enter "X" here* ▶ ☐		
	20A	Unemployment/Supplementary benefit — *Enter the full taxable amount* ▶		
		If part or all of the taxable benefit is included at 5 above, also enter here the amount so included ▶	☐	☐
	21	Widow's and other benefits — Nature of benefit .... *see identity page of Order Book*		
Other pensions	22–23	Pension from former employer and other pensions — Payer's name — Address		
Trade, profession or vocation	1	Nature: FREELANCE WRITER — Business name and address: 34 NEWFIELD ROAD, OLDGATE, LR3 6PT		AS ACCS FOR YEAR TO 30-6-84 8000
	25–27			
	29	Balancing charges and stock relief recovery charges		
	28	Relief for absence on business abroad	Dates of absence *enclose statement where necessary*	
	29	Deduction for capital allowances ... Self £ ... Wife £; Stock relief ... Self £ ... Wife £		
	30	*If exceptionally your profits for Class 4 National Insurance Contributions purposes are affected by interest paid, certain capital allowances or losses not given in the assessment, give details on a separate sheet and enter "X" here* ▶ ☐		

Page 2

SPECIMEN FORM

INCOME: Year 6 April 1984 to 5 April 1985

	See Note	Details			Amount for year	
Property		Address	Gross income including premiums £	Expenses *enclose statement* £	Self £	Wife £
	35	Unfurnished lettings				
	35	Furnished lettings				
	35	Furnished holiday lettings				
	36	Ground rents or feu duties				
	37	Land				
Interest not taxed before receipt		*Enter ALL the interest from each account*				
	38	National Savings Bank } *Including any exempt amount see Note 38* { Ordinary account ... ... ▶				
		Investment account ... ... ▶				
	39	Other banks *enter name of bank* OLDGATE BANK LTD			200	
	40	Other sources (including War Loan, British Savings Bonds and loans to private individuals) OLDGATE BANK LTD FIXED TERM DEPOSIT			1030	
Untaxed income from abroad	41					

	See Note	Name of United Kingdom company	Amount for year: Amount of dividend £	Amount of tax credit £
Dividends from United Kingdom companies and tax credits	42	Self: AS SEPARATE STATEMENT	140	60
		Wife		

	See Note		Self £	Wife £
Other dividends, interest, trust income annuities etc., already taxed	43–46	Source *show each separately. Enter the gross amount for each holding, trust, etc.*		
Interest from United Kingdom building societies	47	Name of society: OLDGATE BUILDING SOCIETY		70

Attach a separate sheet if there is not enough space in a section

Page 3

SPECIMEN FORM

INCOME: Year 6 April 1984 to 5 April 1985

	See Note	Details	Amount for year Self	Wife
Settlements	48	*Include income and capital from settlements, parental gifts etc. and transfers to be treated as your income*	£	£
Payments from estates	49	*Include receipts from estates of deceased persons in Administration*		
Any other profits or income		*Enter the gross amount*		
	50–58	Source *show each separately*		
	58	Maintenance, alimony or aliment received		
	58	Taxable gains on life assurance policies, etc.		

OUTGOINGS: Year 6 April 1984 to 5 April 1985

	See Note	Details	Amount for year Self	Wife
Interest on loans *excluding bank overdrafts* **for purchase or improvement of property**	60–62	**Only or main residence**	£	£
		a. Building Societies — **Society** / **Account No.**		
		Loan at 5 April 1985:– OLDGATE ZL 2396	*The society will advise me of the amount*	
		Loan paid off in year to 5 April 1985:–		
		Please tick if you did not pay under the net interest arrangements (MIRAS) ☐		
		b. All other lenders: **Name of lender** / **Account No.**		
		Enclose an interest certificate if — you paid interest without deducing tax **or** — you calim higher rate tax relief.		
	63	**Let property** — no. of weeks let ▶ ☐		
		—address .... *Enclose certificates*		
Interest on other loans *excluding bank overdrafts*	60, 65	Qualifying loans *Enclose certificates*		
Other outgoings	67	Covenants, bonds of annuity and settlements		
	68	Covenanted payments to charities OLDGATE PARISH CHURCH *Enter Gross amount before deduction of tax*	100	
	69	Alimony, aliment or maintenance		
	70	U.K. property rents or yearly interest paid to persons abroad		

Alterations in untaxed income or outgoings since 5 April 1984

	75	OLDGATE BANK LTD FIXED TERM DEPOSIT OPENED IN SEPT 1984 AND CLOSED IN MARCH 1985

SPECIMEN FORM

CAPITAL GAINS and Development Gains: Year 6 April 1984 to 5 April 1985

	See Note	Details		Self	Wife
Chargeable assets disposed of	76–85	Date of disposal	Description	Amount of gain for year *Distinguish Development Gains* £	£
		SEPT 1984	FORGE COTTAGE AS ENCLOSED COMPUTATION		
	83			10606	
Chargeable assets acquired	86	Date of acquisition	Description	Cost or acquisition value £	£
		MAY 1984	500 MOORFIELD ELECTRICAL LTD SHARES	1000	
		MAY 1984	3000 HIGHFELL PLASTICS LTD SHARES	1600	

CAPITAL TRANSFER TAX

If you have made a gift or other transfer of value you may be liable to Capital Transfer Tax. In some cases transferors are required to deliver to the Capital Taxes Office (**not** the Income Tax Office) an account of transfers they have made (see Note 88) and there are penalties for failure to do so.

ALLOWANCES: Claim for Year 6 April 1985 to 5 April 1986

See Note — ***Before making any claim read the appropriate note***

90 **Married man living with wife or wholly maintaining her**

Wife's Christian or other forenames .... JEAN

If you married after 5 April 1984 please state (a) date of marriage .... (b) wife's former surname ....

93 **Additional personal allowance**

Details of child in respect of whom your claim is made—

Full names of child *surname first*	Child's date of birth Day	Month	Year	Child 16 or over on 6 April 1985, name of university, college or school or nature of training	Does the child live with you?	Is any other person claiming the allowance for the child?

If your wife is unable to look after herself—

What is the nature of her illness or disablement? ....

Is this likely to continue throughout the year ending 5 April 1986? If so *enter "X" in the box* ▶ ☐

91 **Age allowance for persons born before 6 April 1921**

If you or your wife were born before 6 April 1921, *enter "X" here* ... ...▶ ☐

SPECIMEN FORM

ALLOWANCES *(continued)*

See Note	***Before making any claim read the appropriate note***				
94	**Housekeeper** Full names of housekeeper *surname first*	Status of housekeeper *single, married, separated, divorced, widow or widower*	Is the housekeeper living with you?	Relationship *if any*	If the housekeeper is not your relative, is he or she employed by you for that purpose?

95	**Dependent relative** Name and address of dependant	Relationship to you (or to your wife). If "mother" *state whether widowed, separated or divorced*	Dependant's annual income excluding voluntary contributions: State pension or benefit	Other pension	Other income	If not living with you enter the weekly amount you contribute	1. Does any other relative contribute? *"YES" or "NO"* 2. If "YES" enter the weekly amount	Dependant's date of birth	Nature of illness or disablement *if any*
	DOROTHY STEPHENS	MOTHER-IN-LAW WIDOWED	£ 1803	£ NONE	£ NONE	£ 25	1. NO 2. £	9-6-1910	

96	**Son or daughter on whose services you have to depend** Full names of son or daughter *surname first*	Status of son/daughter *single, married, separated, divorced, widow or widower*	1. Is he/she living with you? 2. Do you maintain him/her?	Which of you is aged, or ill or disabled, yourself or your wife?	If aged enter date of birth *Day Month Year*	Nature of illness or disablement *if any*
			1. 2.			

97	**Blind person's allowance** Self or wife	Local Authority with which registered	Date of registration

98	**Death and superannuation benefits**	Name of society, union or scheme	Full contribution for year to 5 April 1985	Portion for death or superannuation benefits
	Friendly Society — combined contribution for sickness and death benefits		£	£
	Trade union subscription		£	£
	Compulsory payments to provide annuities for widows and orphans		£	

99 Life assurance — limits to relief

If in the year ended 5 April 1985 you and/or your wife paid more than

(a) £1,275 in life assurance premiums (including deferred annuity premiums) *enter the total amount paid* ... ... ▶ £ ....

(b) £85 in deferred annuity premiums and compulsory payments to provide annuities for widows and orphans *enter the total amount paid* ... ... ▶ £ ....

100	**Retirement annuity payments** Enter the nature of the trade, profession or vocation or the name of the employer if earnings arise from a non-pensionable employment or office	Name of insurance company etc. or trust scheme	Contract number or scheme membership number	Amount paid in year to 5 April 1985	Amount to be paid in year to 5 April 1986	Enter year of birth	If a special form is required enter "X"
	FREELANCE WRITER	OLDGATE INSURANCE CO	SF 30/20	1000	1000	1938	

Do not forget to sign the declaration on page 1

Page 6

Note

As John and Jean's mortgage is under MIRAS (see Chapter 3) the actual amount of interest paid to the building society during the year was:

	£
Gross interest	2,650
Less: Tax at the basic rate	795
Net payment	£1,855

The band of income up to £15,400 taxable at the basic rate has then to be extended by both the gross building society interest and the charitable covenant in favour of the church as follows:

	£
Income taxable at the basic rate	15,400
Gross building society interest	2,650
Gross covenanted payment	100
	£18,150

(2) Under Schedule D:

		£	£
Jean's freelance profits		10,000	
Deposit account interest			1,280
Less: Allowances and reliefs			
Pension premium	1,000		
Wife's earned income relief	2,005		
		3,005	
Taxable income		£6,995	£1,280
Tax thereon:			
First £1,500/£1,280 at 40%		600.00	512
Next £4,900 at 45%		2,205.00	
Next £595 at 50%		297.50	
Schedule D tax payable for 1984/85		£3,102.50	£512

Class 4 National Insurance Contributions

Profits	10,000
Less: Minimum limit	3,950
	£6,050
Liability at 6.3%	£381.15

	Income Tax	*National Insurance*	*Total*
Payable on 1 January 1985	2,063.25	190.58	2,253.83
Payable on 1 July 1985	1,551.25	190.57	1,741.82
	£3,614.50	£381.15	£3,995.65

Notes

(a) Jean pays tax during 1984/85 on the profits shown by her accounts ending in the previous tax year to 30 June 1983.

(b) The deposit interest which is taxable is made up as follows:

	£
Bank deposit account (previous year)	250
Fixed term deposit (current year)	1,030
	£1,280

(3) Higher rates on taxed investment income

	Gross Income £
Dividends and tax credits	200
Building society interest	100
	300
Tax thereon:	
£300 at 50%	150
Less: Tax deductible at source	90
Tax payable on 1 December 1985	£60

(4) Capital Gains Tax

		£
Sale proceeds of country cottage		24,000
Less: Costs of sale		920
		23,080
Acquisition value	10,000	
Installation of central heating	1,000	
	11,000	
Indexation allowance	1,474	
		12,474
Chargeable gain		£10,606
Tax thereon:		
First £5,600		Exempt
Next £5,006 at 30%		1,501.80
Tax payable on 1 December 1985		£1,501.80

Note

The Retail Price Index was 313.4 in March 1982 and 355.5 in September 1984. The increase in the Index in this period was: (355.5 − 313.4) ÷ 313.4 = 0.134. The indexation allowance is £11,000×0.134=£1,474.

Some tax planning advice for John

(1) In view of the level of John and Jean's taxable earnings for 1984/85 it would benefit them to make an election for Jean's freelance profits to be separately taxed. They have until 5 April 1986 to send the election to the Inland Revenue. It would reduce their total tax payable by over £570 (see Chapter 7).

(2) Jean could pay a larger premium into her personal pension policy. As she was born just before the last War the maximum premium qualifying for tax relief for 1984/85 was £1,750, being $17\frac{1}{2}\% \times$ £10,000 (see Chapter 5).

(3) If John is helping to support Tom while he is studying at university it would benefit him to do so by taking out a deed of covenant in his son's favour (see Chapter 8).
(4) Both John and Jean could have given their daughter Sarah a gift of £5,000 when she married Stephen last November (see Chapter 13).
(5) When John comes to consider reinvesting the proceeds of sale of his country cottage he should consider whether he has sufficient life cover both to protect his family and as an investment. He may also choose to look at some of the types of investment where the return is tax free (see Chapter 6).

TABLE 1

PERSONAL ALLOWANCES AND INCOME TAX RATES FOR 1982/83 AND 1983/84

Personal allowances

	1982/83 £		1983/84 £	
Personal allowance – single	1,565		1,785	
– married	2,445		2,795	
Wife's earned income relief	1,565		1,785	
Age allowance – single	2,070	Income limit of £6,700	2,360	Income limit of £7,600
– married	3,295		3,755	
Additional personal allowance	880		1,010	
Widow's bereavement allowance	880		1,010	
Housekeeper relief	100		100	
Son's or daughter's services	55		55	
Dependent relative relief	100 or 145		100 or 145	
Blind person's relief	360		360	

Income Tax rates

1982/83

Band of Taxable Income £	*Rate of Tax* %	*Tax on Band* £	*Cumulative Tax* £
0–12,800	30	3,840	3,840
12,801–15,100	40	920	4,760
15,101–19,100	45	1,800	6,560
19,101–25,300	50	3,100	9,660
25,301–31,500	55	3,410	13,070
over 31,500	60		

1983/84

Band of Taxable Income £	*Rate of Tax* %	*Tax on Band* £	*Cumulative Tax* £
0–14,600	30	4,380	4,380
14,601–17,200	40	1,040	5,420
17,201–21,800	45	2,070	7,490
21,801–28,900	50	3,550	11,040
28,901–36,000	55	3,905	14,945
over 36,000	60		

Investment income surcharge

1982/83	First £6,250	Nil	Excess	15%
1983/84	First £7,100	Nil	Excess	15%

TABLE 2

INLAND REVENUE EXPLANATORY BOOKLETS

Booklet No.	Title
IR 1	Extra Statutory Concessions
IR 4	Income Tax and Pensioners
IR 4A	Income Tax – Age Allowance
IR 11	Tax Treatment of Interest Paid
IR 13	Wife's Earnings Election
IR 20	Residents and Non-Residents Liability to Tax in the United Kingdom
IR 22	Income Tax – Personal Allowances
IR 23	Income Tax and Widows
IR 24	Class 4 National Insurance Contributions
IR 25	The Taxation of Foreign Earnings and Pensions
IR 27	Notes on the Taxation of Income From Real Property
IR 28	Starting in Business
IR 29	Income Tax and One-Parent Families
IR 30	Separation and Divorce
IR 31	Income Tax and Married Couples
IR 32	Separate Assessment
IR 34	PAYE
IR 37	Income Tax and Capital Gains Tax: Appeals
IR 41	Income Tax and the Unemployed
IR 42	Income Tax: Lay-Offs and Short-Time Work
IR 43	Income Tax and Strikes
IR 45	Income Tax and Capital Gains: What Happens When Someone Dies
IR 47	An Income Tax Form Entitled Deed of Covenant by Parent to Adult Student

IR 51	Business Expansion Scheme
IR 52	Your Tax Office
IR 53	PAYE for Employers
480	Income Tax – Notes on Expenses Payments and Benefits for Directors and Certain Employees
MIRAS 6	Mortgage Interest and Your Tax Relief
P7	Employer's Guide to PAYE
CGT 4	Capital Gains Tax – Owner Occupied Houses
CGT 5A	Capital Gains Tax – Unit and Investment Trusts
CGT 8	Capital Gains Tax (A Comprehensive Booklet)
CGT 11	Capital Gains Tax and the Small Businessman
CGT 12	Indexation
CTT 1	Capital Transfer Tax

TABLE 3

Flat Rate Allowances for Special Clothing and the Upkeep of Tools

(1) Fixed rate for all occupations

	£
Agricultural	45
Forestry	45
Quarrying	45
Brass and copper	65
Precious metals	45
Textile prints	40
Food	25
Glass	40
Railways	40
Uniformed prison officers	35
Uniformed bank employees	25
Uniformed police officers up to and including chief inspector	35

(2) Variable rate depending on category of occupation

Seamen	55/85/110
Iron mining	50/65
Iron and steel	30/40/80

Aluminium	30/40/65/85
Engineering	30/40/65/80
Shipyards	30/40/50/75
Vehicles	25/40/70
Particular engineering	30/40/65/80
Constructional engineering	30/40/50/75
Electrical and electrical supply	15/60
Textiles	40/55
Clothing	20/30
Leather	25/35
Printing	20/45/70
Building materials	25/35/55
Wood and furniture	30/50/60/75
Building	25/35/55/75
Heating	45/60/70
Public service	25/35

Note
The allowances are only available to manual workers who have to bear the cost of upkeep of tools and special clothing. Other employees, such as office staff, cannot claim them.

TABLE 4

RATES OF NATIONAL INSURANCE CONTRIBUTIONS

	1983/84	*1984/85*
CLASS 1 contributions for employees		
Standard rate	9%	9%
Contracted-out rate:		
First £32.50/£34.00 a week	9%	9%
Between £32.50 and £235.00 a week	6.85%	
£34.00 and £250.00 a week		6.85%
Reduced rate for married women and widows with a valid election certificate	3.85%	3.85%
Men over 65 and women over 60	Nil	Nil
Lower earnings limit – weekly	£32.50	£34.00
– monthly	£140.83	£147.33
– annually	£1,689.96	£1,767.96
Upper earnings limit – weekly	£235.00	£250.00
– monthly	£1,018.33	£1,083.33
– yearly	£12,219.96	£12,999.96

CLASS 2 contributions for the self-employed		
Weekly flat rate	£4.40	£4.60
Small earnings exception	£1,775	£1,850
CLASS 3 voluntary contributions		
weekly	£4.30	£4.50

CLASS 4 contributions for the self-employed
1983/84: 6.3% of profits between £3,800 and £12,000
1984/85: 6.3% of profits between £3,950 and £13,000

TABLE 5

THE ALL STOCKS INDEX

	1983	*1984*	*% increase*
January	229.1	242.6	5.90
February	230.5	244.0	5.86
Period of account ending after 12 March 1984 and beginning between			
14 March 1983 and 1 April 1983			6.36
2 April 1983 and 1 May 1983			5.45
2 May 1983 and 1 June 1983			5.00
2 June 1983 and 1 July 1983			4.64
2 July 1983 and 1 August 1983			4.51
2 August 1983 and 1 September 1983			3.71
2 September 1983 and 1 October 1983			3.11
2 October 1983 and 1 November 1983			3.02
2 November 1983 and 1 December 1983			2.93
2 December 1983 and 1 January 1984			2.42
2 January 1984 and 1 February 1984			1.45
2 February 1984 and 1 March 1984			0.87
2 March 1984 and 12 March 1984			0.00

TABLE 6

CAPITAL GAINS TAX – THE INDEXATION ALLOWANCE

Starting month for indexation	*Month of Disposal 1984*								
	Apr	May	Jun	Jul	Aug	Sept	Oct	Nov	Dec
1982									
Mar	.116	.120	.123	.122	.132	.134	.141	.145	.144
Apr	.094	.098	.101	.099	.110	.112	.119	.122	.121
May	.086	.090	.093	.092	.102	.104	.111	.114	.113
Jun	.083	.087	.090	.089	.099	.101	.108	.111	.110
Jul	.083	.087	.089	.088	.098	.101	.107	.111	.110
Aug	.082	.086	.089	.088	.098	.100	.107	.110	.110
Sept	.083	.087	.090	.089	.099	.101	.108	.111	.110
Oct	.078	.082	.084	.083	.093	.096	.102	.106	.105
Nov	.072	.076	.079	.078	.088	.090	.097	.100	.099
Dec	.074	.078	.081	.080	.090	.092	.099	.102	.101
1983									
Jan	.073	.077	.080	.079	.089	.091	.098	.101	.100
Feb	.068	.072	.075	.074	.084	.086	.093	.096	.095
Mar	.066	.070	.073	.072	.082	.084	.091	.094	.093
Apr	.052	.056	.058	.057	.067	.069	.076	.079	.078
May	.047	.051	.054	.053	.063	.065	.071	.075	.074
Jun	.045	.049	.051	.050	.060	.062	.069	.072	.071
Jul	.039	.043	.046	.045	.054	.056	.063	.066	.065
Aug	.035	.038	.041	.040	.050	.052	.058	.062	.061
Sept	.030	.034	.037	.035	.045	.047	.054	.057	.056
Oct	.026	.030	.033	.032	.041	.043	.050	.053	.052
Nov	.023	.027	.029	.028	.038	.040	.046	.049	.049
Dec	.020	.024	.027	.025	.035	.037	.043	.047	.046
1984									
Jan	.021	.025	.027	.026	.036	.038	.044	.047	.046
Feb	.017	.020	.023	.022	.031	.033	.040	.043	.042
Mar	.013	.017	.020	.019	.028	.030	.037	.040	.039
Apr		.004	.006	.005	.015	.017	.023	.026	.025
May			.003	.001	.011	.013	.019	.022	.021
Jun				.000	.008	.010	.016	.020	.019
Jul					.009	.011	.018	.021	.020
Aug						.002	.008	.011	.010
Sept							.006	.009	.008
Oct								.003	.002
Nov									.000

TABLE 7

NON-TAXABLE STATE BENEFITS

Sickness Benefit, Invalidity Allowance and Pension
Addition to Unemployment and Supplementary Benefits in respect of children, housing or special needs
Maternity Allowance and Grant
Death Grant
Attendance Allowance
Family Income Supplement
Industrial Injury and War Disablement Benefits
Mobility Allowance
Child Benefit and other benefits in respect of children
War Widows and Orphans Pension
Job release Allowances under schemes for women aged 59 or over and men aged 64 or over

1985 BUDGET HIGHLIGHTS

Personal allowances and Income Tax rates for 1985/86

The Chancellor has raised both the single and married tax allowances by just under 10%. This is about 5% more than the amount required to compensate for inflation during 1984. The single and married age allowances are going up by the same cash amounts of £200 and £300 as the corresponding single and married allowances. The thresholds at which the higher rates of tax become payable have been adjusted with the movement in the Retail Prices Index during 1984.

Personal allowances 1985/86

	£
Married man	3,455
Single person	2,205
Wife's earned income relief	2,205
Additional personal allowance	1,250
Age allowance — single or widowed person	2,690
— married couple	4,255
— income limit for age allowance	8,800
Widow's bereavement allowance	1,250
Housekeeper	100
Son's or daughter's services	55
Dependent relative	100 or 145
Relief for blind person (each)	360

Income Tax rates 1985/86

Rates of tax applying to all income

Band of taxable income £	*Rate of tax* %	*Tax on band* £	*Cumulative tax* £
0—16,200	30	4,860	4,860
16,201—19,200	40	1,200	6,060
19,201—24,400	45	2,340	8,400
24,401—32,300	50	3,950	12,350
32,301—40,200	55	4,345	16,695
Over 40,200	60		

The PAYE tables will give effect to these changes on the first pay date after 17 May 1985.

National Insurance contributions for employees and employers

From 6 October 1985 employees' and employers' National Insurance contributions will be calculated on a new graduated scale from which the rate of contributions will be determined by the level of earnings. Contributions will then be paid at the same rate on all earnings in accordance with the following table:

	Employee Rate Not Contracted Out %	Employee Rate Contracted Out %	Employer Rate Not Contracted Out %	Employer Rate Contracted Out %
Contributions levied on all weekly earnings if they reach £35.50 but do not exceed £54.99	5.00	2.85*	5.00	0.90*
All weekly earnings if they reach £55.00 but do not exceed £89.99	7.00	4.85*	7.00	2.90*
All weekly earnings if they reach £90.00 but do not exceed £129.99	9.00	6.85*	9.00	4.90*
All weekly earnings if they reach £130.00 but do not exceed £265.00	9.00	6.85*	10.45	6.35*
If weekly earnings exceed £265.00	9.00% of £265	9% on the first £35.50; 6.85% on earnings between £35.50 and £265	10.45% on all earnings	10.45% on the first £35.50 and on earnings in excess of £265; 6.35% on earnings between £35.50 and £265

*Applies only to earnings between the lower and upper earnings limits.

National Insurance contributions payable by the self-employed

Class 2 Contributions

It is proposed that with effect from 1 October 1985 the flat-rate

Class 2 contribution for the self-employed will be reduced from the present £4.75 per week to £3.50 per week.

Class 4 Contributions — Tax Relief

In addition to paying the flat-rate Class 2 contribution, self-employed taxpayers will be liable to National Insurance under Class 4 at the rate of 6.3% of profits above a lower limit of £4,150 and up to a maximum of £13,780 for 1985/86.

The table below shows the amount of Class 4 National Insurance contributions payable for 1985/86 by a self-employed person at various levels of profits and the reduction of Income Tax which will result from the proposed relief. The reduction in tax is that for a married man on the assumption that his income consists entirely of self-employment income taxable at the basic rate of 30%.

Profits	Class 4 N.I. Contribution for 1985/86	Reduction in Income Tax
£	£	£
4,000	—	—
5,000	53.55	8
6,000	116.55	17
8,000	242.55	36
10,000	368.55	55
12,000	494.55	74
14,000	606.69 (maximum)	91

Approved profit-sharing schemes

The Inland Revenue approves profit-sharing schemes which satisfy certain conditions. An employee who is allocated shares under such a scheme is not liable to Income Tax on their value providing he retains them for seven years. When the 1985 Finance Bill receives the Royal Assent this period will be reduced from seven to five years.

Mortgage interest relief

The overall limit on borrowings for the purchase and improvement of the borrower's home up to which the interest is eligible for mortgage interest relief is unchanged at £30,000.

Most borrowers make their regular mortgage repayments after deduction of tax at the basic rate on the interest element in each repayment. This procedure has come to be known as 'Mortgage Interest Relief at Source' – MIRAS for short. Lenders are not at present required to apply these arrangements to loans above the limit of £30,000. If they wish they can elect to do so. The Chancellor proposes to introduce legislation in the Finance Bill which will require lenders to apply the MIRAS arrangements to new loans above the limit with effect from April 1987.

Charitable deeds of covenant

At present an individual is entitled to Income Tax relief at the higher rates on covenanted payments to charities up to £5,000 per annum gross. With effect from 1985/86 this gross limit is to be raised to £10,000 annually.

Business Expansion Scheme

Individuals investing in shares in property-development companies which are issued after 19 March 1985 will not be able to claim relief from Income Tax on their investment under the Business Expansion Scheme. This restriction will not normally affect building and construction companies.

It is proposed to extend the current Scheme to companies carrying on research and development. Relief will apply to shares in such qualifying companies issued after 5 April 1985.

Bond washing

Legislation is being introduced to counter the practice known as 'bond washing'. This is the conversion of income on fixed-interest securities into capital by selling shortly before the ex-dividend date. As a result the accrued income, which is received as capital, is chargeable to Capital Gains Tax rather than Income Tax.

The legislation will treat interest on fixed-rate investments as accruing on a day-to-day basis between payment dates. On a sale, the accrued interest from the previous payment date to the date of the transaction will be charged to the vendor's Income Tax. The purchaser will be allowed to deduct this amount from the interest which he receives on the following payment date. These charges and deductions will be excluded from Capital Gains Tax calculations.

These arrangements will cover both fixed and variable-rate stocks and bonds including those issued in a bearer form. Both U.K. and overseas fixed-interest investments issued by governments, companies, local authorities or other institutions and whether secured or unsecured are included. Excluded will be ordinary and preference shares, National Savings Certificates, certificates of deposit, bills of exchange, Treasury and local authority bills, or other similar instruments.

The new rules will apply to all taxpayers except those where the nominal value of their securities is under £5,000 at any time.

The new rules will apply on or after 28 February 1986. There are transitional provisions covering the period until the commencement of the accrued-income scheme.

Reform of personal taxation

Later this year the Chancellor of the Exchequer will publish a consultative Green Paper on the reform of personal income tax. It will discuss a number of options for the Income Tax system. These range from taxing the incomes of a married couple separately to closer integration between the tax and benefit systems. One particular possibility is a restructuring of the personal allowances under which each individual would be entitled to a single personal allowance. It would be set against their own income. If husband and wife were unable to use part or all of their allowance they would be able to transfer it to their partner. The incomes of a married couple would no longer be added together in calculating their Income Tax liability. Married women would be afforded the possibility of complete privacy and independence in their tax affairs.

The Government aim to phase in the new system over a period of years. It appears that legislation is intended in 1987 so that the new system could be fully operational from April 1990.

Capital allowances

The 1984 Finance Act phased out first-year allowances completely by 31 March 1986. All items of plant and machinery acquired after that date will only attract 25% annual writing-down allowance on a reducing balance basis. This will allow 90% of the cost of the machinery and plant to be written off for tax purposes over eight years.

It is proposed that where taxpayers expect within five years to dispose of an item of machinery or plant acquired on or after 1 April 1986 at less than its tax written-down value, they will be able to elect to have capital allowances on such items calculated separately from the main machinery or plant pool. This is to be known as 'de-pooling'.

Writing-down allowance for plant or machinery will now be available when expenditure is incurred whether or not the equipment has been brought into use. This change will take effect in respect of chargeable accounting periods ending on or after 1 April 1985.

Value Added Tax

The limit at which it is necessary to register for VAT is increased to outputs of £19,500 p.a. (previously £18,700 p.a.). The quarterly registration limit is also increased to £6,500 from £6,200.

Application for cancellation of registration for VAT will be possible from 1 June 1985 where predicted future turnover is not expected to exceed £18,500 p.a. inclusive of VAT (previously £17,700). Also, a person who has been registered for at least two years may apply for cancellation of registration after 1 June 1985 if his turnover (inclusive of VAT) in each of the preceding two years has not exceeded £19,500, and if he does not expect his turnover to exceed this figure in the following year.

Business gifts
The limit is raised from £2 to £10 which a business may spend on promotional gifts to any one person in the course of a year and this expenditure allowed for tax purposes against business profits. The new limit will apply to expenditure incurred after 5 April 1985.

Capital Gains Tax
The amount of an individual's gains in the tax year exempt from Capital Gains Tax is to be raised from £5,600 to £5,900. For the purposes of the £5,900 exemption the gains made by husband and wife will continue to be aggregated.

The rate of Capital Gains Tax remains unchanged at 30%.

Retirement relief gives individuals exemption from Capital Gains Tax on gains of up to £100,000 on the disposal on retirement of business assets or shares or securities in a family business. It was previously given to persons aged 65 or over, with tapering relief for those aged between 60 and 65. The £100,000 relief will now apply at 60 with no tapering relief. It is proposed that individuals who retire early for reasons of ill health will also be entitled to the relief.

The following changes are proposed to the rules relating to the calculation of the indexation allowance in respect of disposals by individuals on or after 6 April 1985.

(a) The allowance is now to apply to both expenditure on acquiring an asset and enhancing its value from the time that expenditure is incurred or March 1982 if later. Ownership of the asset for a minumum period of 12 months before it qualifies for the allowance is no longer necessary.

(b) The allowance will now be given in the case of losses and it will be possible for a gain to be turned into an allowable loss.

(c) Where assets were acquired before 6 April 1982 by an individual, the indexation allowance will be calculated by reference to the market value at 31 March 1982 where this value is greater than the actual cost incurred.

Under the proposed legislation on bond washing, that part of any sale or purchase price taken into account as income in the new proposals will be excluded from the sale proceeds or acquisition costs for Capital Gains purposes. Gains on sales of government stock and qualifying corporate bonds will continue to be exempt from Capital Gains if held for more than 12 months.

Capital Transfer Tax

It was provided in the Finance Act 1982 that the rate bands would be adjusted in line with the changes in the Retail Price Index on an annual basis. No other changes to the rates are proposed, the relevant increase in the Index being 4.58%. The proposed rates (from 6 April 1985) are shown in the following tables.

Rates of Capital Transfer Tax on Gifts made during Lifetime

Proposed Rates (From 6 April 1985 inclusive)

Band £	Rate %	Tax on Band £	Cumulative Tax £
0– 67,000	0	Nil	Nil
67,001– 89,000	15	3,300	3,300
89,001–122,000	17.5	5,775	9,075
122,001–155,000	20	6,600	15,675
155,001–194,000	22.5	8,775	24,450
194,001–243,000	25	2,250	36,700
243,001–299,000	27.5	15,400	52,100
Over 299,000	30	—	—

Rates of Capital Transfer Tax on Death

Proposed Rates (From 6 April 1985 inclusive)

Band £	Rate %	Tax on Band £	Cumulative Tax £
0– 67,000	0	Nil	Nil
67,001– 89,000	30	6,600	6,600
89,001–122,000	35	11,550	18,150
122,001–155,000	40	13,200	31,350
155,001–194,000	45	17,550	48,900
194,001–243,000	50	24,500	73,400
243,001–299,000	55	30,800	104,200
Over 299,000	60	—	—